POWER POSE

Mastering a Leadership Presence for Women

by

RACHEL BROOKS

CONTENTS

INTRODUCTION:
EMBRACING THE POWER OF PRESENCE

In the dynamic world of leadership, there's a subtle yet powerful force that can distinguish a good leader from a great one—the power of presence. Leadership presence isn't just about the way you communicate; it's the energy you exude, the command you have over your emotions, and the aura you carry into every interaction. It's that magnetic quality that inspires others to follow, to believe, and to achieve. It is both an art and a science, a blend of observable actions and internal mindset.

Women who aspire to leadership positions often face a unique set of challenges, but with those challenges come incredible opportunities. Forging a path in leadership is about skill, certainly, but it also encompasses the gravitas that comes from a leader's very being. Understanding and cultivating your presence is essential for rising to the occasion and fully embracing the role of leader in any workplace.

Presence is not merely a static state; it's a dynamic process of engagement with the world around you. It's about how you enter a room, how you can captivate an audience without saying a word, or how you can encourage and inspire with just a glance. It embodies the confidence you carry within yourself, not just in moments of triumph but also in times of trial.

There is, however, no one-size-fits-all approach to building your leadership presence. It's a personal journey that combines your unique strengths with learned skills, an understanding of social dynamics, and the wisdom of emotional intelligence. Leadership presence is about harnessing your personal power and amplifying it to lead others effectively.

As we embark on this journey together, you'll discover how to define and refine your own leadership style, leveraging your innate qualities to make a lasting impact. You'll learn the critical elements that contribute to a leader's presence, from body language to dress, and from vocal delivery to emotional savvy.

Stepping into a leadership role is more than assuming a title; it's about embodying the very essence of guidance and direction. The power of presence enables you to not only lead with conviction but to also evoke trust and respect from your team. It's about creating a positive and enduring influence that transcends the constraints of hierarchy.

It's important to note that presence isn't about dominance or intimidation. Instead, it's about the authentic expression of your best self in service of leading others. You'll find that leadership presence is intrinsically linked to values such as integrity, authenticity, and empathy. It's these qualities that engender the true respect of your peers and subordinates alike.

Throughout the pages to come, you will engage with cutting-edge research in the fields of psychology and management. Simultaneously, you'll revisit timeless insights from leaders who have exemplified the power of presence. Their stories and experiences will illuminate the path as you apply these lessons to your own leadership journey.

Moreover, embracing the power of presence means recognizing and tapping into the wealth of potential that resides within. It's a power that builds over time, requiring patience, practice, and a mindset geared toward continuous growth. As a woman in leadership, your presence is a beacon that can guide your team through uncertainty and success alike.

You'll learn to communicate not just with words, but with every fiber of your being. Each gesture, each choice of clothing, each inflection in your voice contributes to the story you tell as a leader. By mastering these elements, you'll gain the ability to move and motivate others toward shared goals in a way that is powerful and palpable.

However, mastering presence isn't just about influence—it also involves resilience. Your journey as a leader will undoubtedly encounter obstacles and setbacks. Embracing the power of presence will equip you with the grace to stand firm amidst challenges, leading with a calm and steady hand. It will enable you to bounce back with renewed vigor and insight—qualities that define resilient leadership.

The power of presence also extends to forming and nurturing professional relationships. Strategic networking, authentic connections, and the dynamic of mentorship all play a role in shaping your leadership narrative. It's about creating an ecosystem where you can thrive, contribute, and help others to do the same.

Decision-making is another aspect where your presence can make a tangible difference. A leader's choices often set the tone for their team and organization. Thus, imbuing your decisions with confidence and clarity, while remaining open to insights and input, can forge a path of security and certainty for all who follow.

Your presence is much more than a tool for achieving immediate objectives; it's a legacy you build with each day's efforts. It's the mark you leave on your team, your organization, and the broader landscape of leadership. As we explore the many facets of presence in this book, remember that you're not just learning skills, but crafting the very essence of your contribution as a leader.

You stand at the threshold of transformation — an opportunity to embrace the formidable, exquisite power of presence. It's time to unfold the marvels of your leadership as you evolve, inspire, and lead. Together, we'll explore the vast realms of presence and discover how you can use it to shine as a beacon of progress, poise, and power.

CHAPTER 1:
DEFINING LEADERSHIP PRESENCE

Leadership presence isn't just about the title you hold; it's the essence that you bring to the table. It's the unmistakable amalgam of confidence, poise, and authenticity that can captivate a room and inspire teams to excel. For women ascending the leadership ladder, mastering this dynamic quality is more than a nice-to-have—it's a crucial part of the executive footprint. In this pivotal chapter, we'll unwrap the core components that formulate this magnetic attribute. You'll learn how a commanding presence is often the deciding factor in effective leadership and why understanding its elements is the first step in your journey. While we'll delve into body language, wardrobe, and communication in later chapters, here we lay the foundation, drawing the blueprint for a presence that's both felt and remembered—igniting a spark to transform potential into reality and positioning you at the helm of change with grace, strength, and vision.

The Elements of Presence

In the journey towards impeccable leadership, there's one intangible trait that universally stands out: presence. You know it when you see it—the leader who walks into a room and instantly commands attention, exuding confidence, clarity, and charisma. We often wonder if presence is innate or can be cultivated. In this chapter, we delve into the constituting elements of presence and unwrap the tapestry that makes a leader not only seen but felt and remembered.

Presence is not a one-dimensional attribute, but rather a tapestry woven from various threads. One of the most crucial threads is **confidence**. Confidence isn't about never feeling uncertain; it's about the bravery to move forward despite uncertainty. Leaders with presence show a steadfast belief in their mission and convey a vision that inspires others to follow. They stand firm in the face of adversity and express their thoughts without hesitation or doubt.

Another fundamental aspect is **clarity**. A leader's message must be clear and articulate, allowing their vision and direction to resonate with others. Clarity includes the ability to distill complex ideas into an essence that ignites passion and motivates. It's not just what you say; it's how you say it—the ability to convey complex strategies in ways that are easily digestible and actionable.

Alongside clarity, there's the mastery of **communication**. A present leader knows that dialogue is a two-way street, conversing with empathy and openness. They are adept at reading between the lines and sensing the unsaid emotions and thoughts in a conversation. Their communication style bridges gaps and fosters a deep sense of connection and understanding among their teams.

The ability to remain **composed** amidst turmoil is also central to a leader's presence. This composure is less about emotionlessness and more about emotional control. It's about facing challenges without getting visibly rattled, thus providing a pillar of stability for all those who look up to you for guidance and reassurance.

An integral component of presence is **authenticity**. This means leaders are true to their values, ethics, and beliefs, and their actions align with their words. Authenticity builds trust, and a leader who is trusted becomes a magnetic north that others willingly follow. They're not interested in putting on acts but instead show their genuine selves, even when it means being vulnerable.

Presence is also supported by **attentiveness**. A leader who listens actively and intently to others demonstrates respect and value for their team's input. Attentiveness isn't merely about giving someone your time; it's about engaging fully and making others feel seen and heard.

A leader's **adaptability** can dramatically impact their presence. The capacity to adjust your style in response to different situations and individuals signals a flexible mindset and a leader prepared to take on the unexpected. It's a dynamic approach to leadership that says, 'Come what may, we will find a path forward.'

Fostering **inclusivity** adds depth to a leader's presence. When leaders celebrate diversity and cultivate an environment in which all voices have a platform, they weave a rich, diverse tapestry of perspectives into the decision-making process and the culture of their organization.

Of course, presence is underpinned by **emotional intelligence** — the ability to navigate the emotions of oneself and others with finesse. Emotionally intelligent leaders can build rapport and trust swiftly and sustainably by understanding the undercurrents of emotional exchanges.

The energy a leader brings into a space is also a telltale sign of their presence. There's an elusive quality to **energy** — it encompasses enthusiasm, passion, and the vigor to propel people and projects forward. Leaders with presence radiate a contagious energy that infuses their work environment with dynamism and fervor.

Presence is not void of **tact and diplomacy**. Leaders who demonstrate presence handle sensitive situations with grace, avoiding unnecessary offense. They are skilled in delivering difficult messages and navigating complex interpersonal dynamics without diminishing their integrity or compromising their relationships.

Lastly, there is the aspect of **grace under fire**. When the pressure mounts, leaders with true presence maintain their grace. They face critical, high-stress situations with a level-head and a clear strategy, showing those around them that every challenge is surmountable.

The amalgamation of these elements results in a presence that is far more powerful than the sum of its parts. It's a delicate balance between strength and sensitivity, courage and caution, action and introspection. In the following chapters, you'll learn how to assess and refine these elements within your own leadership style, enhancing not just how you are perceived, but also how effectively you lead.

As we move forward, remember that presence is not a static state but a dynamic and evolving attribute. Continuous reflection and dedication to your personal leadership development will refine your presence. Each interaction you have is an opportunity to project your leadership presence, to embody the qualities that make a remarkable leader, and to step into your power fully and authentically.

In essence, mastering the elements of presence is mastering the art of being compellingly you, in the most impactful way. It's a constant journey of self-improvement and adjustment as you respond to new challenges and lead with increasing grace and effectiveness. Keep these elements in mind as we proceed, they are the building blocks of your path to one day becoming that leader who, simply by entering a room, can transform it entirely.

Assessing Your Current Leadership Style

To carve out a space where you can be a transformative leader, you must first understand the foundation upon which you'll build your presence. Assessing your current leadership style isn't just about introspection; it's an essential step in identifying the strengths you can draw on and the areas where growth is not just possible, but necessary. Discover your leadership baseline and you're on your way to crafting an authentic and compelling presence.

Begin by reflecting on feedback you've received in your career. Often, how others perceive us holds critical clues into our leadership style. Do colleagues describe you as assertive and decisive, empathetic and nurturing, or innovative and visionary? These descriptors shine light on the energy you bring to a team and the impact you have on your work environment.

Self-assessment tools can also offer valuable insights. There are myriad assessments available that gauge everything from decision-making styles to conflict resolution. Consider taking a few to get a composite view of your leadership qualities. These tools can provide a quantitative baseline that, combined with qualitative feedback, forms a well-rounded picture of your leadership style.

Reflection is often most powerful when it's focused. Take a moment to look back at specific instances that challenged your leadership skills. Maybe it was a project that went off course or a team conflict that needed resolving. What actions did you take? What did these actions reveal about your inherent leadership approach?

Contemplate your communication style, too. Effective leaders are known not just for what they say, but how they say it. Analyze conversations you've had with your team. Are you more directive or do you encourage dialogue? Your communication style greatly influences team dynamics and can either foster an environment of open collaboration or stifled creativity.

Your emotional intelligence (EI) plays a pivotal role in leadership. Being attuned to your own emotions and those of others allows you to navigate workplace relationships with sensitivity and insight. Reflect on a time when emotions ran high at work. How did you manage your feelings and the feelings of others? Your response in these moments is telling of your EI as a leader.

Consider your approach to conflict. Do you seek harmony at all times, or are you comfortable leaning into the tension if it means arriving at a better solution? Leadership presence isn't about avoiding conflict but about managing it with poise and integrity. Your conflict resolution style can either inspire trust or erode it.

Take a holistic view of your leadership style by assessing your comfort with risk. Leaders who nurture a strong presence often display confidence in their decisions, even in uncertainty. Do you lean into challenges and embrace innovation, or do you find comfort in tradition and the tried-and-true? Neither is better, but knowing where you stand can highlight areas for growth and arenas where you're likely to excel.

What's your method for decision-making? A reflective leader examines both past successes and failures when facing new choices. Scrutinize situations where you had to make tough calls. Did you feel equipped to make those decisions, or were there gaps in knowledge or confidence that impeded you? This analysis is essential for understanding the degree to which your decision-making style aligns with a solid leadership presence.

Peer into how you build and cultivate relationships in a professional setting. Leaders who leave a lasting impression tend to be skilled at networking, often expanding their influence beyond immediate circles. How do you foster these connections? Are you passive, waiting for opportunities to arise, or are you proactive, seeking out relationships that can support your leadership journey?

The manner in which you set goals and drive progress reveals much about your direction as a leader. Are your targets ambitious, but achievable? How do you approach setbacks? An effective leader leverages obstacles as stepping stones to future success, demonstrating resilience and adaptability.

Finally, whether you're managing projects or people, your style of leadership boils down to your influence—how you motivate and empower those around you. Influence is the currency of leadership presence. Think about times you've persuaded your team to get on board with a new idea. What strategies did you utilize? Reflect on your persuasiveness and the subtle ways you enact change.

Your leadership style is a tapestry woven from your experiences, attributes, and choices. By diligently assessing where you are today, you set the stage for where you aspire to be tomorrow. Envision the leader you want to become, and use this thorough self-assessment as your launching pad. You already have the raw materials of a great leader within you; now it's time to hone and highlight them.

Embrace the knowledge that leadership presence is a skill that can be developed. It's not an inborn trait but a quality that is crafted and refined over time. As you work through this self-assessment, remember that every great leader had a point of departure. Your journey is unique, and the insights you gain today will inform the leader you'll grow into—resilient, influential, and poised to change the world.

Let this assessment be not an end, but a beginning. As you move forward, you'll find that leadership is less about mastery and more about perpetual growth and learning. Let your findings guide your transformation and approach each day as a new opportunity to embody the leadership presence that is uniquely yours.

CHAPTER 2:
THE SCIENCE OF BODY LANGUAGE

As we pivot from understanding the essence of leadership presence, it's imperative to delve into the granular science underpinning body language. The nuanced choreography of non-verbal gestures carries a symphony of unspoken narratives that can make or break the perception of a leader. This chapter unpacks the silent yet potent language spoken through every stance, hand movement, and eye contact; a language that transmits confidence, empathy, and decisiveness without uttering a single word. Mastery of this art form is crucial for aspiring leaders, as body language forms the cornerstone of commanding respect and anchoring your presence in the collective consciousness of your team. By decoding the complex lexicon of physical expression, you'll uncover powerful pathways to influence and connect, magnifying your leadership persona in ways that words alone simply can't achieve. Thus, let's harness the silent eloquence of body language and translate its hidden power into actionable presence.

Communication Beyond Words

In the intricate dance of leadership, the unspoken signals you transmit can be just as telling as the words you choose. Your body language is a potent instrument of communication, woven into the fabric of your interactions, shaping your presence without a whisper. As you advance in your journey to become an inspiring leader, it's crucial to master the art of silent dialogue. Grasping the subtle art of non-verbal expressions—be it the confidence radiated by a steady gaze during a negotiation, or the warmth conveyed by an open posture during a team meeting—empowers you to connect profoundly with your audience. Each nuance of your gestures, each micro-expression on your face, contributes to the narrative of your leadership. These wordless cues serve as a dynamic undercurrent, reinforcing your messages and evoking responses more profound than spoken language ever could. By sharpening your awareness and control over your body's own lexicon, you'll unlock new dimensions to guide your team, not just with dictation, but with the charismatic force of unspoken eloquence that resonates with every heart and mind in the room.

The Role of Non-Verbal Cues in Leadership

In the grand tapestry of communication, words are but one thread that contributes to the overall image. As emerging leaders, women have a cache of tools at their disposal, and among the most impactful of these is the art of non-verbal communication. Non-verbal cues can often say more than spoken words, offering a silent orchestra of messages that can lead, inspire, and forge connections in the workplace. This intricacy and richness are what makes mastering non-verbal communication a cornerstone of effective leadership.

Take a moment to consider the gravity of body language in conveying authority and approachability. A leader's physical presence, from posture to eye contact, can set the tone for interaction before a single word is uttered. When you enter a room with a straight spine and maintained eye contact, you're not just occupying space – you're commanding it. Your body speaks volumes to your team, often translating to an aura of reliability and confidence that can be as effective as an articulate speech.

Facial expressions, too, are a potent component of non-verbal communication. A genuine smile can be a universal sign of warmth, often breaking barriers and fostering an environment where ideas flow freely. Conversely, an unintended frown or puzzled look might inadvertently create distance or uncertainty. As a leader, your awareness and control of your facial expressions are vital in ensuring that you are always sending the intended message.

Gestures can equally be double-edged swords. Consider the impact of open versus closed gestures. When you speak with hands open and palms visible, you project honesty and willingness to engage. On the other hand, crossed arms might be perceived as a defensive stance, possibly putting others on guard. Learning to use gestures to complement your message rather than distract or contradict it is an art that enhances your overall impact as a leader.

The subtlety of touch, while often overlooked, can be another powerful non-verbal tool. A simple pat on the back or a firm handshake can convey a sense of trust and solidarity. Of course, it's essential to understand and respect personal and cultural boundaries, but appropriate and consented touch can humanize and strengthen leader-team connections.

Silence, often underestimated, is another key non-verbal aspect. Knowing when to pause can add weight to your words and give others the space to contribute. This practice not only demonstrates confidence in your message but also shows respect for the opinions and thoughts of your team. Mastering the power of the pause can transform an average interaction into a dynamic exchange of ideas.

Proximity is an often overlooked aspect of non-verbal cues. The physical distance you maintain during interactions can influence the perceived intimacy and intensity of the engagement. Leaders who are adept at managing this dynamic can create an atmosphere that's collaborative when the situation calls for teamwork or more authoritative when decisive action is needed.

The cadence of your movements should not be ignored. Leaders who move intentionally, without haste or nervousness, exude composure and thoughtfulness. This careful orchestration of movement can demonstrate a leader who is deliberate and in control, qualities admired and followed.

Incorporating non-verbal cues effectively also means aligning them with your spoken words. Congruence between what you say and how you say it reinforces trust. When your body language is in sync with your verbal messages, it amplifies your credibility and authenticates your commitment to your role as a leader.

It's also crucial to be attentive to the non-verbal cues of others. A leader who can read the room and respond to the team's silent signals is poised to address concerns, foster collaboration, and mitigate conflicts before they escalate. Your ability to interpret and react to non-verbal signals can make the difference between a harmonious work environment and one fraught with misunderstandings.

To refine this skill, self-awareness is key. It begins with observing not only how others perceive your non-verbal cues but also how you perceive yourself. Are you projecting the image you wish to convey? Video recording your practice sessions or asking for honest feedback can provide valuable insights into your non-verbal communication style.

While self-awareness is the foundation, adaptability is the strategy. Different situations and audiences may require shifts in your non-verbal communication. Being rigid in your non-verbal approach can be as limiting as using only one type of leadership style. Adaptability ensures that your non-verbal cues remain effective and relevant across various contexts.

Inspiring and leading a team involves more than just setting a vision – it's about embodying that vision through every gesture, every expression, and every posture. As you grow as a leader, continually refine your non-verbal communication skills. They are your silent partners in persuasion, motivation, and inspiration.

The mastery of non-verbal cues is a lifelong journey, but it begins with intentionality. Start by incorporating one non-verbal element into your leadership practice at a time, be it maintaining eye contact, using positive gestures, or mastering the strategic pause. Through practice and persistence, these elements will become second nature, allowing your leadership presence to shine brightly.

Embrace this silent language and let your non-verbal cues speak volumes about your leadership capabilities. Remember, your presence – how you stand, how you move, how you listen – can dramatically augment your influence and impact as a leader. Through honing this intricate craft, you will not only inspire but also empower those around you to reach their highest potential. This is the non-verbal symphony of leadership, silent yet powerful, an embodiment of leadership excellence.

Decoding Gestures and Postures

The art of interpreting body language opens a window into understanding leadership dynamics. As aspiring leaders, it's crucial to decipher the subtle messages conveyed through gestures and postures. These nonverbal cues can speak volumes about a person's confidence, openness, and authority.

Imagine walking into a room and spotting someone with their arms folded tightly across their chest. You might instinctively feel that the person is closed off or defensive. This is a stark example of how our brains are wired to read body language as a survival mechanism. In leadership, this intuition can help us navigate the countless subconscious conversations happening around us.

Leadership presence isn't just about the words you say but also about how your body communicates your conviction and poise. Slouching or fidgeting can inadvertently suggest a lack of confidence, while an upright posture projects strength. Posture isn't just about standing tall; it's about embodying the leadership role you aspire to fill.

Gestures can be equally powerful. Consider the difference between pointing a finger, which can feel accusatory, versus an open-palmed gesture, which is seen as inviting and inclusive. Leaders use their hands to emphasize points, but the way you use this tool can impact your audience's reception of your message.

A handshake, for instance, is often the first physical interaction in a professional setting. A firm, steady handshake can set the stage for a relationship built on respect, while a limp or overly forceful handshake might create an unfavorable impression. Mastering this simple gesture can make a significant difference in first impressions.

Mirroring is another aspect of body language that can be quite influential. When you subtly mimic the postures and gestures of those you're interacting with, it can create a rapport and show empathy. Be cautious, though, as overdoing it can seem disingenuous. The key is to strike a balance and use mirroring to build connections naturally.

Consider the power stance: feet planted firmly on the ground, hands on hips, standing tall. This pose not only affects how others see you but can also change how you feel about yourself. Embracing such postures before important meetings or negotiations can bolster your confidence and presence.

Eye contact is an integral part of your body language repertoire. When you maintain appropriate eye contact, it can signal engagement and honesty. In contrast, avoiding someone's gaze might suggest deceit or disinterest. Striking the right balance in eye contact can create a connection and demonstrate your leadership focus.

Facial expressions also convey a wealth of information. A genuine smile can be disarming and warm, encouraging others to see you as approachable and cooperative. On the other hand, a furrowed brow might express concern or deep thought. Learning to manage your facial expressions can help you better align your nonverbal signals with your leadership intent.

Physical space and how you occupy it can further augment your leadership presence. Leaders who use space wisely, not aggressively, can exude authority without saying a word. Knowing when to lean in or step back during a conversation can enhance the impact of your verbal communication.

It's important to remember that context matters. A gesture that's positive in one culture could be offensive in another. As a leader in today's global business environment, you must be culturally aware and sensitive to the nonverbal norms of different societies.

Interpreting the gestures and postures of others is just one side of the equation. You also have to be aware of your own body language. Regularly practicing in front of a mirror or recording yourself in simulated leadership scenarios can help you become more conscious of your nonverbal cues and improve them over time.

Lastly, while understanding body language is powerful, it's also important not to jump to conclusions based on a single gesture or posture. Nonverbal cues need to be read in clusters and in relation to the situation. Effective leaders learn to observe patterns in body language to comprehend the complete message being communicated.

Incorporating the science of body language into your leadership style isn't about manipulating your gestures and postures to exert influence falsely. It's about aligning your nonverbal communication with your values and goals as a leader. When your body language is congruent with your spoken words, you present a compelling and authentic leadership presence.

Keep honing your ability to decode gestures and postures, and watch how it transforms not only the way others perceive you but also how you perceive yourself. Your journey to leadership is enriched by these subtle yet profound skills that allow you to communicate and lead with greater impact.

CHAPTER 3:
THE ART OF THE POWER POSE

As we delve into the core of commanding a room, let's explore the transformative potential of power poses. The way you carry yourself speaks volumes before you even utter a word. It can exude confidence, elevate your state of mind, and even alter your body's chemistry. Imagine standing tall, shoulders back, chin lifted—feeling invincible. But it's more than just finding a pose; it's about embodying the poise that tells the world you're a formidable leader. Think of it as a silent dialogue with those around you, where you channel the grace of a ballerina and the unwavering stability of a skyscraper, intertwined. Engaging in this physical expression of self-assurance isn't merely for effect; it's a practice rooted in psychological research, one that can bolster your presence in both the boardroom and beyond. Each time you adopt this stance, it's like stepping into an invisible suit of armor. Remember, your body is an instrument of your intent—learn to play it with majestic finesse, and the symphony of leadership will resonate in every gesture you make.

Finding Your Signature Stance

In the world of leadership, your physical presence speaks volumes before you've even uttered a word. Establishing your signature stance is an integral step in harnessing the power of non-verbal communication and conveying confidence. This stance isn't just a posture; it's a reflection of your inner strength and leadership identity. It's a position that becomes synonymous with your presence in any room, signalling to others that you're a force to be reckoned with.

Finding your signature stance involves a journey of self-discovery and awareness. You'll need to experiment with different postures to identify what feels most natural and empowering for you. Remember, there's no one-size-fits-all in the art of the power pose. What resonates with your authenticity will likely differ from that of another leader. Your stance should be a blend of comfort and assertiveness, a balance that says you're accessible yet unshake-able.

Begin by standing in front of a mirror and observing how you naturally distribute your weight. Do you lean more on one foot? Is your head held high, or do you find your gaze naturally drifting downward? Make a conscious effort to stand with your feet shoulder-width apart, grounding yourself firmly. This base offers stability and is a classic power posture that promotes balance and openness.

Once you've found a balanced stance, cultivate a sense of openness. Let your arms hang comfortably by your sides or place your hands on your hips if that feels more powerful. The goal is to create space between your arms and your body; this openness signifies that you are not afraid to take up space and that you welcome interaction.

Your shoulders carry the burden of tension, so be mindful of them. Roll them back to open up your chest, and then relax, ensuring they're not hunched up around your ears. This positioning showcases a confident bearing, inviting respect and attention from your peers. It's a physical manifestation of readiness and competence.

The tilt of your head can project authority as well. Keeping your chin parallel to the floor conveys a level-headedness and engagement with your environment. Direct eye contact is a tool of the confident leader; when paired with your signature stance, it speaks of your attention to detail and respect for others.

As you refine these elements, incorporate dynamic movements that are in sync with your signature stance. This can include gesturing with your hands to emphasize points during a conversation or stepping forward when greeting a colleague. Movement adds vitality to your stance, ensuring that while it is your default, you are never perceived as rigid or statuesque.

Throughout this process, it's essential to maintain breath control. Effective leaders don't hold their breath; they breathe deeply from the diaphragm. This type of breathing fuels your voice, delivering your words with clarity and strength.

It's also important to be mindful of your environment and adapt your stance accordingly. For instance, sitting at a negotiating table requires a different approach – feet flat on the ground, hands visible, and seated tall with your back straight. Adaptability doesn't mean compromising your presence; it means fitting the power of your signature stance to the context you're in.

Stillness can be a powerful component of your stance. In high-pressure situations, resisting the urge to fidget or constantly adjust your posture can show remarkable composure and self-assurance. Embrace moments of stillness as opportunities to display a calm, commanding presence.

Notice the sensation of confidence as it begins to grow with practice. A signature stance isn't just for appearances; it can have a profound effect on your mind too. Don't be surprised if you start to feel more in control and decisive as you reinforce your signature stance regularly.

As you move towards making your signature stance a natural part of your leadership style, solicit feedback. Ask trusted colleagues or mentors how your posture affects their perception of you. This feedback can offer valuable insights that help you fine-tune your presence.

Beyond reflection and feedback lies the realm of consistency. Implement your signature stance consistently across different settings to establish it as a hallmark of your leadership. Whether you're standing to address your team or walking into a high-stakes meeting, your consistent stance ensures that you are instantly recognized and respected.

Lastly, while finding your signature stance is essential, it's part of a broader spectrum of your leadership development. Integrating this stance with effective communication, emotional intelligence, and strategic thinking cultivates a comprehensive leadership presence that will set you apart and propel you forward. Practice this stance until it feels like second nature, until it becomes a permanent emblem of your leadership identity.

Remember that as a leader, your journey is continually evolving. Your signature stance today may adjust as you grow and face new challenges. Embrace this flexibility, for it is in the nuances of your evolving stance that your leadership story unfolds. Stand tall, stand proud, and watch as your signature stance opens doors to new possibilities and successes.

Practice Makes Permanent

You've discovered your signature stance, the position that makes you feel undeniably powerful and ready to take on the world. But how does this pose become more than just a temporary feeling? How does it integrate into your very being? The answer lies in the simple, timeless adage: practice makes perfect. But here, we're aiming for more than perfect. We want permanence, a state where your power pose isn't just a strategy, but a natural part of your leadership embodiment.

Consider for a moment the way expertise is developed in any skill. Does a pianist play a complex concerto flawlessly on their first attempt? They do not. It takes countless hours of practice, where the movements of their fingers over the keys become so ingrained that they need not think about each note. Instead, the music flows out of them. You must approach your power poses with the same dedication and repetition to turn them into an instinctive part of your presence.

Begin by setting aside time each day to practice your power pose. It's important that this isn't done half-heartedly. The practice should be intentional and focused. Stand in front of a mirror, embody your pose, and take notice of how you feel. Make adjustments as needed to ensure you're conveying the presence you desire. Note your posture, your facial expressions, and the sense of confidence emanating from you. These sessions do not need to be lengthy; even a few minutes each day can have a profound impact over time.

Document your progress. This could be through journaling or even taking photos or videos of your practice. Reflection is key to improvement. Reviewing your documentation will help you recognize the changes in your body language, and consequently, in your self-perception and confidence.

Integrate your power pose into your daily routine. Practicing doesn't mean you only stand in front of a mirror. It means assuming your power pose before meetings, during conversations, and in moments of solitude. Let it become a natural part of your stance whenever you need to feel grounded and assertive.

Visualize your success. Imagine yourself in high-stakes situations, maintaining your power pose with ease. Visualization is an immensely powerful tool used by athletes and high-performance professionals worldwide. It prepares your mind and body to act accordingly when the situation arises.

Incorporate feedback into your practice. Seek the opinions of trusted friends, mentors, or coaches on your body language. Ask them what they perceive when you are in your power pose and take their observations seriously. They might notice subtleties that you have missed which can help refine your pose further.

Remember that consistency is vital. Practicing sporadically will not lead to the solidification of your power pose in your leadership presence. It must be a regular endeavor. Dedication to your practice is as important as the practice itself. Over time, muscle memory and mental association will kick in, transforming your pose from something you do to something you are.

Be patient with yourself. Progress may be incremental and not immediately obvious. Every great change is the culmination of many small shifts. Celebrate the small victories, as each one is a step towards making your power pose a permanent aspect of your leadership presence.

Engage in mindfulness. Part of making your power pose permanent is understanding the internal shifts that come with it. Being mindful of your mental state while in your pose can fortify the connection between the physical and psychological aspects of your power.

Adapt and evolve. Your power pose, while becoming a fixed part of your presence, should not be rigid. As you grow in your career and as a leader, allow your pose to evolve with you. It may need tweaking as your responsibilities and environments change, and that's okay.

Overcome setbacks with resolve. There will be days when assuming your power pose may feel awkward or unnatural. This is especially true when facing challenges or setbacks. It's in these moments that your practice becomes particularly crucial. Push through the discomfort, for it's in these instances that your true strength is forged.

Finally, link your practice to a cue, a specific situation, or time of day. This forms a habit loop, where the cue triggers the action – your power pose – which in turn creates a reward: the empowering feeling you get from it. The more you engage in this loop, the more ingrained your power pose will be in your daily leadership.

Your leadership journey is uniquely yours, and how you carry yourself physically will influence not only how others perceive you but also how you perceive yourself. By making deliberate effort to practice, you are not just developing a powerful skill; you're investing in the embodiment of your leadership potential. Practice doesn't just make perfect; in the realm of presence, practice makes permanent. And it's within this permanence that your true power lies.

Transitioning into the next chapter of your leadership development journey, remember the strength and poise you've cultivated through diligent practice. All of these traits will coalesce to dress you not just in the attire of success but in the undoubted confidence that comes from knowing your presence is powerfully permanent.

CHAPTER 4:
DRESSING FOR SUCCESS

As we pivot from the empowering practice of power poses, we delve into the transformative potential of attire in **Dressing for Success**. Your wardrobe is a dynamic tool that, when managed thoughtfully, can reinforce your leadership presence and communicate your professional narrative without saying a word. Think of your clothing as an extension of your leadership identity, each garment a thread in the fabric of your visual storytelling. Whether it's the boldness of a blazer that contours your ambition, or the strategic choice of a silk blouse that whispers your approachability, the clothing you choose can be as compelling as your body language. This chapter isn't just about fashion—it's about curating a sartorial repertoire that aligns seamlessly with your leadership objectives. *How can you exude confidence and competence while remaining true to your unique style?* By harnessing the nuances of color theory and the subtleties of style, we'll navigate the spectrum of workplace attire to create a wardrobe that's not only professionally appropriate but imbued with intentionality, making every step you take a reaffirmation of your leadership journey.

Aligning Your Wardrobe with Your Leadership Goals

When we consider the powerful intersection between personal style and leadership, wardrobe alignment stands out as a crucial area for reflection and strategic action. For women poised to climb the leadership ladder, the way you dress communicates volumes before you even speak. It's an outward expression of your competence, confidence, and ambition. In this section, we'll delve into how to meticulously align your wardrobe with your leadership goals, crafting an image that not only resonates with who you are but also projects where you're headed.

The process of wardrobe alignment begins with a clear understanding of your leadership goals. What is the essence of the message you wish to convey? Are you aiming to project strength, innovation, approachability, or perhaps a blend of these attributes? Each goal may dictate a slightly different sartorial approach but remember that consistency is key. Establish a coherent personal style that aligns with the leadership traits you want to exemplify.

Leadership is not just about the role; it's about the story you tell and how people perceive you. Your wardrobe is a powerful tool for storytelling. If your goal is to be seen as an innovator within your industry, then incorporating modern, forward-thinking elements into your attire could convey this narrative. Think sleek silhouettes, bold patterns, and smart, tech-friendly accessories that signify a forward-looking mindset.

Conversely, if your leadership journey is steering towards roles that demand gravitas and command respect, traditional styles with a contemporary twist can convey that balance of authority and relatability. This doesn't mean staid or dull; it means choosing classic pieces that are tailored impeccably to your form and that speak to a sense of timeless quality.

For those aiming to underscore their approachability and teamwork ethos, outfits that blend professional with personable can strike the right chord. Incorporating softer colors, mixed textures, and perhaps even a tasteful accessory that hints at your personal story or passions can create a more accessible demeanor.

While style is subjective, certain universal principles can guide your wardrobe choices. Fit is the foundation of any powerful wardrobe. Even the most expensive suit can't compensate for poor fit—clothes that hug and hang in all the right places catalyze confidence, which in turn enhances your leadership aura. Invest in a good tailor and prioritize the fit over brand or trend.

Cultivating a signature look can be your visual calling card. Perhaps it's a notable watch, a specific cut of blazer, or a trademark color you wear routinely. This consistent element of your attire becomes a part of your personal brand, making you more memorable and reinforcing your leadership presence.

Balance is also vital. Mixing textures, colors, and layers should be done with a thoughtful eye towards creating an overall cohesive look. You want to be remembered for your leadership and ideas, not for a clashing outfit that distracts from your message.

It's essential to consider context within your wardrobe choices. Different industries and companies have varying expectations around attire. What might be considered leadership-appropriate in a creative agency could differ wildly from that in a law firm. Understanding these nuances and adapting your wardrobe to fit these expectations, while still staying true to your own style, reflects a leader who is both self-aware and astutely perceptive of her environment.

Adaptability is significant as you navigate different settings, from boardrooms to casual work functions. Having a versatile wardrobe that can easily transition with a few adjustments means you're prepared for any professional scenario. This adaptability also reflects a flexible leadership mindset, an essential trait in today's dynamic workspaces.

The power of accessories should not be underestimated. They can make a statement, offer a pop of color, or add polish to your ensemble. However, they should be chosen with intention. Each piece, from your shoes to your bag to your jewelry, should serve a purpose and contribute to the story you're telling about your leadership.

Do not forget the importance of grooming and maintenance. Well-cared-for clothes and accessories demonstrate attention to detail—a quality that speaks volumes in leadership. It also depicts respect for oneself and one's role, setting a standard for those you lead to follow.

Transitions in leadership roles can necessitate wardrobe shifts. As you grow and take on new challenges, your wardrobe should evolve accordingly. Regularly assess and update your wardrobe to ensure it remains aligned with your current position and the leadership image you aim to project.

As a woman in leadership, embracing the totality of your identity—including how you present yourself through your wardrobe—is empowering. It transcends the superficialities of fashion, tapping into the authentic expression of your personal brand and the aspirational aspects of who you aim to become.

Ultimately, aligning your wardrobe with your leadership goals isn't just about dressing for the job you want; it's about embodying the leader you are and aspire to be. With every carefully chosen garment, you aren't just covering a body—you're uncovering potentials, setting standards, and inspiring change. Let your wardrobe be a testament to your leadership narrative, a daily reaffirmation of your goals, and a visual cue to the world of the leader within you, stepping forward with every polished, purposeful stride.

Color Psychology and Style Strategy

Within the realm of leadership, the visual impact of your attire is more than a superficial detail; it's a powerful tool that can convey authority, approachability, and confidence. The strategic use of color psychology and style can reinforce your leadership presence and potentially influence the perception of colleagues and stakeholders. As you finesse your wardrobe to align with your leadership goals, understanding the symbolism of color and the nuance of style is essential.

Colors often carry subconscious meanings and can evoke specific emotions in those around us. For instance, the color blue is commonly associated with trust, stability, and serenity, making it an excellent choice for leaders who wish to project a sense of dependability. On the other hand, red can symbolize power and passion but may also be perceived as aggressive if overused. The judicious use of bold hues, combined with more neutral tones, can create a balanced look that commands attention without overwhelming an audience.

Considering the industry in which you lead, color choices may vary. In creative fields, brighter, more vibrant colors can signify innovation and originality. Contrastingly, in more traditional sectors such as finance or law, conservative shades such as grey or navy may convey the professional seriousness you wish to communicate. However, even in conservative environments, a pop of color can add a personal touch that distinguishes you and makes you more memorable.

Understanding and embracing your unique style is just as important as color selection. The clothes you wear should not only represent your role and the culture of your organization but should also make you feel authentically you. Whether your personal style is classic, modern, or eclectic, ensure you're comfortable and confident in your attire as this self-assurance will shine through to those around you.

The cut and fit of your clothing are pivotal. A well-tailored outfit exudes professionalism and polish. Pay attention to how your clothes fit your body type and make alterations as necessary. Clothing that is too tight or too loose can be distracting and may detract from the content of your contributions in the workplace.

Accessorizing is yet another facet of your style strategy. Accessories can be powerful in punctuating your intended message. A statement necklace or a unique timepiece can serve as a conversation starter, while subtle jewelry can add an air of sophistication and detail to your ensemble.

When building your leadership wardrobe, versatility is key. Invest in quality pieces that can be mixed, matched, and layered to create multiple looks. This approach offers you a variety of outfits that can be adapted to different situations, from day-to-day leadership tasks to high-stakes meetings or public speaking engagements.

The context of each situation should also inform your wardrobe decisions. What you wear to an internal team meeting may differ from the ensemble you choose for a public keynote speech. Having a versatile wardrobe allows you the flexibility to adjust your outfit to the formality of the occasion and the expectations of the audience.

It's also wise to consider the psychological effect of certain styles and garments. A blazer or structured jacket, for instance, can immediately elevate your appearance and create an aura of authority. Moreover, investing in timeless pieces rather than chasing fast fashion trends shows an appreciation for quality and a focus on long-term value — both admirable leadership traits.

Beyond color and style, the fabrics and textures you choose to wear can send a message as well. Silk, wool, and other natural fibers can project a sense of luxury and meticulousness, while synthetic fabrics may not carry the same gravitas. The tactile aspect of your wardrobe can enhance the overall impression you make and ensure you're not only seen but also felt as a leader with substance.

The manner in which you care for your clothing also matters. Regular laundering, pressing, and mindful storage all contribute to maintaining a pristine appearance. Your management of these details can be indicative of your overall approach to your work — orderly, thorough, and respectful.

Lastly, remember that authenticity should be the cornerstone of your color psychology and style strategy. Let your wardrobe be an extension of your leadership identity, reflecting your values, capabilities, and vision. When your external presence aligns with your internal character, you create a cohesive and compelling leadership persona.

Above all, approach your leadership wardrobe with intention. Each time you prepare for your day, consider the messages you are sending through your choices. A strategic approach to dressing for success doesn't just enhance how others perceive you; it amplifies the confidence you carry within, and this assurance is the hallmark of a true leader.

By harnessing the psychology of color and curating a style that is uniquely yours, you set the stage for a potent leadership presence. Your wardrobe becomes an integral part of your personal brand, one that can inspire, influence, and make an indelible impact on your path to leadership excellence. Aspire to dress not for the position you hold, but for the leader you are becoming.

CHAPTER 5:
VOCAL MASTERY FOR LEADERS

Stepping away from the attire that frames your presence, Chapter 5 delves deep into the harmony of vocal mastery—a skill that every influential leader wields with precision. The voice is not merely a tool for communication; it is an instrument of power that, when finely tuned, commands attention, exudes confidence, and resonates with the hearts and minds of your audience. As women in leadership, it's imperative to recognize that how you articulate your vision can be just as impactful as the vision itself. This chapter demystifies the nuances of speaking with authority and clarity, guiding you to harness the power of tone and tempo to captivate your listeners. Through strategic modulation and purposeful pauses, leaders can elevate their speech, transforming every conversation into an opportunity to inspire change and drive action. Embrace the strength in your voice, and let it carry your message with unwavering conviction, leaving a lasting impression on those who look to you for direction and inspiration.

Speaking with Authority and Clarity

As leaders, the ability to articulate your vision with conviction and precision is paramount. It's the bridge that connects your inner intent with the outer world's understanding. Speaking with authority and clarity not only heightens your influence, it signifies command over your domain and engenders trust in your leadership.

Authority in speech is not about volume; it's about the confidence with which you present your ideas. To embody this, anchor your statements in certainty. You can practice this by stating your opinions as facts, rather than suggestions. Instead of saying, "I think we should," assert with "We will." Even subtle shifts in language can greatly impact the reception of your message.

Clarity, on the other hand, requires you to simplify complex ideas into accessible language. Leaders who master this craft become beacons of insight, turning the intricate into the understandable. Engage in the discipline of distillation—boil down your ideas to their essence before presenting them. This ensures that your message is not clouded by unnecessary jargon or convoluted reasoning.

Breathing, often overlooked, plays a critical role in speech. Controlled breathing helps regulate your tone and pace. Practice deep, diaphragmatic breaths before speaking, allowing yourself to speak from a place of centeredness. Your voice will carry further with less effort, and your calm will be contagious.

To heighten authority and clarity, focus on enunciation. Mumbling or running your words together can quickly undermine your expertise. Dedicate time to vocal exercises that target diction, making each word you speak distinct and comprehendible.

Pacing is equally important—it adds dynamism to your speech. Rapid-fire delivery can overwhelm listeners, while a monotonous rate can lull them into disengagement. Strive for a tempo that carries energy yet allows for reflection. Pausing before key points can alert your audience to pay closer attention.

Structure your speech logically. A well-organized presentation facilitates understanding. Begin with an overview, delve into details as needed, and conclude with a strong summary that reinforces your central message. This scaffolding is not just for formal presentations but can be applied to everyday communication.

The art of storytelling should not be underestimated. Anecdotes humanize you and illustrate points in ways that raw data never can. Incorporate relevant stories into your communication to captivate and illuminate, but always keep them aligned with your message.

The power of the question cannot be overstated. It engages the audience, prompts self-reflection, and fosters an interactive atmosphere. Use questions to punctuate your discourse, inviting others into a shared space of exploration.

Feedback is a precious tool in sculpting your authoritative voice. Seek out trusted colleagues or mentors to review your speaking patterns. Constructive criticism can reveal habits that obscure your clarity, such as filler words or tangential rambling.

Mentally, envision speaking to the back of the room or beyond the person furthest away from you. This visualization naturally adjusts your projection, ensuring your message reaches everyone. It also subconsciously boosts your confidence, reinforcing the aura of leadership.

Technological tools offer valuable support. Applications that analyze speech patterns provide insights into areas such as pitch, volume, and clarity. Embrace these tools to fine-tune your vocal delivery, but ensure they enhance rather than distract from the authenticity of your voice.

Empathy in language fosters connection. Your message is better received when it considers the perspective and emotions of your audience. Adapt your speech to resonate with those you are addressing, without diluting your core message.

Finally, consistency in your communication solidifies your image as a leader. Let the qualities of authority and clarity permeate not just formal addresses but every interaction. Over time, this consistency becomes synonymous with who you are as a leader.

Your voice is a powerful instrument in the orchestra of leadership. Remember that speaking with authority and clarity is a skill honed over time. Give yourself permission to grow, to stumble, and to rise again with renewed eloquence. Your journey to vocal mastery is a testament to the leader you are and aspire to become.

The Power of Tone and Tempo

As we've previously explored the critical aspects of leadership presence and the role of body language, it's now time to delve deeper into the nuances of vocal mastery. Mastering the tone and tempo of your voice is not just about what you say—it's how you say it that can keep your team engaged, emphasize your message, and exude confidence. Whether you're giving a presentation, negotiating a deal, or delivering feedback, the power of your voice is an essential tool in the leader's toolbox.

Tone and tempo are two vocal elements that are intertwined with the emotions and messages we convey. The tone of your voice can paint a picture, telling your colleagues not just the content of your message but also the emotional landscape behind it. It can express urgency or calm, joy or seriousness, approachability or authority—often all within the same conversation. Mastering your tone means learning to adapt to the needs of the moment, ensuring your voice aligns with the impact you aim to achieve.

Let's start with tone. The tone is often thought of in musical terms, and rightly so. Just as musicians use different tones to evoke different feelings, so too can you modulate your vocal tone to enhance your communication. A lower, measured tone can denote seriousness and authority; it commands attention. Alternatively, a higher-pitched, varied tone can invoke excitement and passion. Remember, it's less about altering your voice to something that feels inauthentic, and more about amplifying what is already there to better serve your purpose.

Now, consider tempo—the speed at which you speak. A deliberate, slow tempo encourages listeners to hang onto every word, creating a sense of importance and weight. On the flip side, a quicker tempo can convey enthusiasm and energy. Leaders must be deft in switching tempos, knowing when to slow down for reflection or to allow emphasis to sink in, and when to hasten the pace to drive a point home or spark action.

But how does one wield these vocal tools effectively? Practice is essential. Experiment with different tones and tempos to see how they affect others' perception of your message. Perhaps record yourself and note the variance in response when you adjust these factors. This ability to self-evaluate and fine-tune your voice is a marker of vocal mastery.

Exercise is also key to mastering tone and tempo. Much like a singer or actor trains their voice, leaders can benefit from vocal exercises to increase control and range. Techniques such as breath control, articulation drills, and pitch exercises not only improve vocal strength but also enhance clarity and expressiveness.

Strategic use of pauses is another essential aspect of tempo control. A pause can be powerful, giving your audience a moment to process a key point, or providing you with a moment to gather thoughts and navigate a challenging question. In the busy hum of the workplace, silence stands out. Mastering the strategic use of silence will distinguish you as a thoughtful and impactful communicator.

Consistency in voice can add to your personal brand. The tone and tempo you consistently employ will become a signature part of your presence. Over time, your team will come to recognize, understand, and trust your vocal delivery, making your communication all the more effective.

That said, maintaining vocal variation is crucial to keeping your audience engaged. A monotone voice, no matter how consistent, can quickly lead to disengagement. Varying your tone and tempo according to the context or the portion of your speech adds dynamism to your delivery, keeping your listeners invested and attentive.

It's also vital to be mindful of cultural nuance when it comes to vocal expression. What might be considered assertive and confident in one culture may be perceived as aggressive in another. Being a global leader means adapting your vocal strategies to diverse audiences, ensuring your message is received with the resonance you intended.

Emotional intelligence plays a significant role in vocal mastery. A strong leader reads the room and adjusts their tone and tempo accordingly. If your team is feeling stressed, a calm and soothing tone can reassure and encourage them. If morale is low, a brisk and buoyant tempo can uplift and energize. The key to this adaptability is keen observation and empathy.

When it comes to pacing, it's not just about the speed of your words, but also the rhythm of your entire speech. The ebb and flow of your message should align with your desired outcome. Think of your speech as a journey where your tempo helps to navigate the terrain—sometimes you'll move swiftly over the flat plains of general information, and other times you'll slow as you climb the steep hills of complex ideas.

In meetings and negotiations, the ability to modulate tone and tempo becomes especially crucial. A well-timed shift in tone can demonstrate your flexibility or resolve, while a calculated change in pace can draw attention to your key points, keeping your audience focused on what matters most.

To conclude, never underestimate the influence of how you say something. While the content of your message is indispensable, the way you deliver it can make all the difference between a forgettable conversation and a memorable one that inspires action and confidence. As you cultivate your leadership presence, let the mastery of tone and tempo be your allies, shaping the perceptions of those you lead and reinforcing your position as a formidable leader.

Empower yourself to use your voice not just as a means of communication, but as an instrument of leadership. With every word you speak, enjoy the symphony you create and the impact it has. Let your voice be the wand with which you conduct the orchestra of your team, guiding them to harmony and success.

As we progress through this journey of vocal mastery, remember that the power of your voice is a reflection of your inner strength and leadership capabilities. Keep honing this craft, for it will serve you well in all corners of the professional sphere, enlightening, influencing, and leading with the poise and assurance that only a true leader can emanate.

CHAPTER 6:
EMOTIONAL INTELLIGENCE IN LEADERSHIP

As we delve into the pivotal role of emotional intelligence in leadership, we uncover a dimension of leadership that can transform your personal impact in the workplace. Emotional intelligence, the keystone of effective leadership, embodies the ability to recognize, comprehend, and manage not only your own emotions but also those of the people you lead. It's about being acutely aware of the undercurrents of interpersonal dynamics and harnessing this insight to foster a positive work environment. This chapter will guide you through the steps of developing your emotional intelligence to enhance your influence and presence as a leader. We'll explore how to read the emotional landscape of your team, respond with sensitivity and understanding, and build empathetic connections that promote trust and respect. Embrace this transformative skill and watch as it amplifies your effectiveness, allowing you to lead with finesse and heartfelt confidence that inspires others to follow.

Understanding and Managing Emotions

As we delve deeper into the journey of leadership, we recognize that the cornerstone to emotional intelligence is our ability to understand and manage emotions—not only our own but also those of others. It is this intrinsic aspect of leadership that allows for the cultivation of healthy work environments and nurtures strong, collaborative teams.

Understanding emotions begins with self-awareness. As a leader, you must be adept at recognizing your emotional triggers and the subsequent responses these provoke. Are you aware of how stress affects your decision-making? Can you identify when you're operating out of frustration rather than logic? Self-awareness provides the clarity needed to navigate complex interpersonal dynamics effectively.

Once you're tuned into your emotions, it's vital to manage them proactively. This doesn't mean suppressing feelings. Rather, it involves acknowledging them and determining the best course of action. For example, feeling impatient with a team member who's struggling might be natural, but expressing that impatience can be counterproductive. Instead, consider ways to provide support and encourage growth.

Managing emotions encompasses emotional regulation—staying calm under pressure and maintaining a positive outlook in the face of challenges. As a leader, your emotional state sets the tone for your team. When you exhibit optimism and resilience, these qualities can inspire your team, thereby enhancing overall morale and productivity.

Emotional intelligence also involves recognizing and appropriately responding to the emotions of others. Empathetic leaders are skilled in understanding the perspectives and feelings of their team members. This empathy builds trust and respect, creating a foundation for strong working relationships. It empowers individuals to open up, share innovative ideas, and contribute meaningfully to the organization's success.

Improving your emotional intelligence means actively listening and providing feedback that demonstrates that you value your team's input. It requires patience and a sincere desire to understand the motivations and concerns of those you lead. Listening isn't just about hearing words—it's about comprehending the emotions that drive the conversation.

Conflict is inevitable in any workplace. How you manage and resolve disagreements speaks volumes about your leadership. Approaching conflicts with a level head and an intention to understand all sides of the issue will often lead to more effective solutions. Managing emotions during these times helps to defuse tension and fosters a culture where issues can be discussed openly and resolved constructively.

An essential aspect of managing emotions is maintaining an open line of emotional communication. Encourage your team to express their feelings and concerns, ensuring that they understand their voices are heard and valued. This transparency can prevent misunderstandings and build a foundation for mutual respect and collaboration.

At times, managing emotions may require you to provide feedback or address negative behavior. The goal is to do so without damaging self-esteem or morale. Frame your feedback in a way that focuses on the behavior, not the person, and offer constructive guidance on how to improve.

It's equally important to celebrate successes—both large and small. Recognizing and sharing these moments boosts the positive emotional climate of the team. Celebrations foster a sense of achievement and acknowledgment, which are strong motivational factors.

Mindfulness and reflective practices can enhance your ability to understand and manage emotions. Taking time for self-reflection helps you stay connected with your emotional state and allows you to address any areas of concern before they impact your leadership.

As you progress in your leadership journey, remember that managing emotions is not a fixed target but a continuous process. It involves constant learning and adapting. It pays to stay curious and open to personal growth, as your emotional intelligence directly influences your effectiveness as a leader.

Moreover, in leadership, few things are done alone. Your ability to understand and manage emotions within a team context is paramount. This may involve facilitating emotional intelligence workshops or team-building activities that focus on enhancing these skills across your unit.

In conclusion, understanding and managing emotions is crucial in your role as a leader. The empathy, patience, and emotional regulation that you demonstrate can inspire your team and contribute greatly to organizational success. As you enhance these skills, you'll likely find that both your professional and personal relationships will benefit, allowing you to navigate the complexities of leadership with confidence and grace.

Embracing emotional intelligence in leadership does more than just foster a positive workplace; it projects a personal brand of authenticity. When your team sees you as a leader who values and manages emotions effectively, they will mirror those behaviors, promoting a culture of emotional awareness and self-regulation. This is how you truly leave an indelible mark in the corporate landscape as a leader of distinction.

Building Empathetic Connections

In the journey to leadership excellence, understanding and navigating the intricacies of human emotion are pivotal. Perhaps the most delicate and powerful thread in the fabric of leadership is the ability to build empathetic connections. Empathy is the beacon that guides the way to mutually respectful and understanding work relationships, illuminating the path to true collaboration and inclusiveness.

For aspiring women leaders, mastering empathy is not about nurturing a soft presence; it's about demonstrating a formidable strength. Empathy allows you to tune into the emotional wavelength of those you aim to lead, offering insights into their motivations, fears, and aspirations. These insights, when acknowledged and appreciated, foster an environment where trust thrives and collective goals are pursued with passion and determination.

Empathy in leadership begins with active listening: giving full attention to the speaker without the distraction of forming a response. It's about truly hearing the concerns and ideas of your team members. This attentive stance signals respect and valuing of their contributions, encouraging openness and discouraging workplace silence where issues lurk unaddressed.

It's crucial to remember that empathetic leadership also involves being attuned to non-verbal communication. Just as we've discussed the significance of body language, being able to read the unspoken signals of others serves as a silent conversation where much is said. Acknowledging a team member's reluctance or hesitation through their body language can steer the discussion in a way that reveals hidden challenges.

As leaders, we must never underestimate the power of vulnerability. A leader who shares their own challenges and setbacks opens the door for others to do the same. This shared vulnerability becomes the bedrock of a supportive culture where learning from failure is not only acceptable but encouraged, fostering a collective strength in the face of adversity.

Empathy means cultivating patience and understanding the uniqueness of each person's journey. Some members on your team will excel under pressure, while others may require a different approach to unlock their full potential. An empathetic leader recognizes these individual needs and adapts their style to nurture growth in everyone.

Emotional intelligence in leadership isn't about ignoring the hard decisions or the necessity of providing critical feedback. Quite the contrary, it's about delivering this feedback in a compassionate manner that focuses on improvement and problem-solving, rather than blame. This creates a learning opportunity rather than a moment of defeat.

An empathetic leader knows that recognition goes a long way. It's essential to celebrate not just the big wins, but also the small but significant steps individuals take towards the team's goals. This reinforces a positive narrative that each contribution is valuable and meaningful to the collective effort.

Framing problems as shared challenges is another hallmark of an empathetic leader. By characterizing obstacles as collective endeavors, you reinforce communal bonds and emphasize a culture where every team member plays a crucial role in the solution. You're not just leading a team; you're building an empowered community.

Building empathetic connections also means being deliberate about inclusivity. Fostering environments where diverse thoughts and experiences are not only heard but sought after is critical. A leader adept in empathy champions a space where every voice matters, shaping policies and cultures that reflect this ethos.

To further understand the impact of empathy in leadership, consider seeking feedback from peers and subordinates about your empathetic actions. Constructive criticism will help fine-tune your empathetic approach, solidifying your skill of understanding different perspectives and emotional states.

Remember to also reflect on your team's dynamics. Are there patterns of interaction that could be improved with empathy? Perhaps there's an undercurrent of stress or dissatisfaction that, if addressed with a compassionate ear, could transform the working environment and propel productivity.

Finally, imbue daily interactions with small acts of empathy. Whether it's a thoughtful question about a colleague's well-being or showing genuine interest in their weekend activities, these gestures have a compounding effect, reinforcing the emotional bonds that underpin effective leadership.

The role of an empathetic leader extends beyond the confines of the office. It's about building bridges that connect the personal with the professional, demonstrating a leadership approach that respects the holistic nature of individuals. You're not just investing in your team's professional success, but in their emotional well-being.

As you continue to navigate your leadership journey, remember that the power to inspire, influence, and effect change is significantly amplified by your ability to connect emotionally. Empathy is not just a leadership tool; it's a powerful testament to the humanity within leadership—a quality that not only enriches the workplace but transforms lives.

CHAPTER 7:
STRATEGIC NETWORKING FOR CAREER GROWTH

In the quest for ascension within the elusive echelons of leadership, strategic networking emerges not just as an asset but a cornerstone of career growth. This chapter dives deep into how you can build a formidable and resourceful professional network that serves as a launchpad for leadership opportunities. Strategic networking goes beyond exchanging business cards; it is about cultivating meaningful professional relationships that foster mutual growth and learning. We'll explore techniques for identifying and nurturing key contacts, and provide actionable insights on how to approach professional alliances with confidence and poise. Learn to recognize the symbiotic nature of mentorships and sponsorships, and how these dynamics can profoundly impact your journey. Networking isn't just about who you know; it's about who knows you and the value you bring. By mastering the art of networking, you ready yourself to step into the limelight, accruing allies who support and amplify your leadership capacity. Your network can be your greatest advocate, propelling you toward your career goals with wisdom, strength, and grace.

Cultivating Professional Relationships

As you navigate the exciting and multifaceted landscape of career advancement, remember that relationships are the fertile soil from which opportunities blossom. Cultivating professional relationships is a nuanced dance, balancing authenticity with strategy; it's about connecting on a personal level while maintaining a professional aim. Begin by actively listening and engaging in conversations that showcase your genuine interest in others' passions and challenges—it's in these moments that true connections are forged. Foster these relationships with careful nurturing through follow-up emails, offering your expertise, or a simple note of gratitude. Be generous with your network, understanding that the power of a strong professional relationship often lies in the mutual benefits it can provide. By approaching networking with a spirit of collaboration rather than competition, you'll create a web of connections that not only uplifts you but can also propel you towards those coveted leadership roles. Engage, support, and be prepared to learn— with every interaction, you're not just building a network; you're cultivating the very foundations of your future as an inspiring leader.

Mentorship and Sponsorship Dynamics

As we transition from the importance of strategic networking, it's critical to delve deeper into the underpinnings of mentorship and sponsorship within professional settings, especially for women aspiring to leadership positions. At their core, mentorship and sponsorship are about relationships that can fuel career advancement, but they are distinct in their functions and impact.

Mentorship is often considered the bedrock of professional growth. A mentor provides guidance, shares knowledge, and imparts wisdom from their wealth of experience. Importantly, as a woman in pursuit of leadership, identifying a mentor who aligns with your aspirations and values can make a significant difference. A good mentor not only offers advice but also listens, providing a sounding board for your ideas and concerns. They can also introduce you to new ways of thinking and help you navigate the complexities of workplace dynamics.

In the context of mentorship, the dynamic is typically one-on-one, with sessions that are introspective and strategy-oriented. A mentor can illuminate paths you may not have considered and can help you learn from their trials and triumphs. Ideally, this relationship is built on mutual respect and trust, which takes time and consistency to establish.

While mentorship is invaluable, sponsorship plays a different yet complementary role. A sponsor is someone who not only advises but also actively advocates for you within the organization or industry. This advocacy is crucial. A sponsor uses their influence to help you secure high-profile projects, promotions, and opportunities that might otherwise be inaccessible.

The dynamics of sponsorships are more overtly strategic and often involve more significant risks for the sponsor. They are putting their reputation on the line to open doors for you. As such, the reciprocity in this relationship is clear: you must demonstrate your competence and potential to not only benefit from the relationship but also to uphold and enhance your sponsor's credibility.

Understanding these dynamics empowers you to leverage these relationships effectively. Knowing when to seek counsel from a mentor and when to leverage a sponsor's influence can be pivotal in a career. Both are integral to career acceleration but serve different purposes: mentors refine your skills and acumen while sponsors amplify your visibility and advocate for your advancement.

Building these relationships requires that you first understand your own goals and capacities. Knowing what skills and competencies you need to develop will inform the type of mentorship you seek. Conversely, understanding your strengths and potential contributions will make you more attractive to potential sponsors.

Moreover, while these dynamics can significantly influence your professional trajectory, they are not static. The guidance you need at one stage of your career will differ from another, just as a sponsor who is instrumental in one phase may not be the best advocate in the next. Flexibility and introspection are needed to cultivate these relationships as you grow.

Additionally, there's also power in becoming a mentor or sponsor yourself. You can create virtuous cycles of support within your network, enhancing not just your own leadership capabilities but also contributing to the growth of others. This dual role of receiver and giver of support magnifies your impact and helps build a more robust professional community.

Fostering these relationships is not without its challenges. One must navigate these dynamics with emotional intelligence, recognizing and respecting boundaries, and ensuring that all parties benefit. Efforts must be directed towards building authentic connections rather than transactional ones, as the latter may not withstand the tests of time and change.

Tapping into the potential of mentorships and sponsorships also means becoming comfortable with vulnerability. It involves asking for help, expressing ambitions, discussing shortcomings, and sometimes, weathering disappointments. Such experiences, while daunting, are part of the growth process and can lead to significant breakthroughs.

When seeking out mentors or sponsors, one should approach with sincerity, preparedness, and clear intentions. It's important to articulate what you're looking for in the relationship, whether it's specific advice, exposure to new challenges, or connections to other professionals. Clarity from the outset ensures the relationship starts on the right foot and is geared towards tangible outcomes.

In closing, the mentorship and sponsorship dynamics are a rich soil from which your leadership capacities can grow. They are resources that provide not only guidance and opportunities but also inspire confidence. Their impact on your journey can be profound, acting as catalysts that accelerate your path to leadership.

As you advance and redefine your leadership presence within your industry, remember that these relationships are as much about contributing to others' growth as they are about receiving support. Balance is key; your rise through the ranks can, and should, lift others as you climb. Mentorship and sponsorship are not merely stepping stones but also the very threads that connect and strengthen the tapestry of tomorrow's leadership landscape. Embrace them with intention and gratitude, and you will find yourself not only climbing the ladder of success but also crafting a legacy of leadership that echoes beyond your personal achievements.

Navigating Social Events with Confidence

As you've cultivated a strong foundation in leadership presence, body language, and professional wardrobe strategies, you now stand at the gateway of another pivotal aspect of career growth: navigating social events with confidence. Social events can range from casual office gatherings to structured industry conferences, each offering a unique opportunity to solidify your role as a burgeoning leader and connector in your field.

First, it's essential to recognize that confidence is not an inherent trait but a skill that can be developed with practice and intention. Approaching social events with a mindset geared towards learning and growth can transform nerves into excitement, opening doors to valuable connections and experiences.

Preparation is your ally when it comes to attending social events. Prior to the event, research the attendees, if possible, and identify who you want to connect with. This will help you to focus your time and give you conversation starters that are relevant and engaging. Knowing your audience and having a game plan eases anxiety and ensures that you make the most of your time.

Upon arriving, use your body language to project approachability. A genuine smile, open posture, and direct eye contact invite others to engage with you. The power poses you've practiced can also come in handy to give you a pre-event boost of confidence. Remember that your non-verbal cues often speak louder than words.

Dressing for success, as discussed in a previous chapter, also plays a critical role in how you are perceived. Choose attire that is appropriate for the occasion and makes you feel empowered. This amplifies your confidence and allows you to focus on interactions rather than being self-conscious about your appearance.

Your voice, too, is a powerful tool. Speak with clarity and conviction, using the vocal mastery skills you've honed to leave a lasting impression. Practice active listening, which not only shows respect but also provides valuable insights into the needs and interests of those you are engaging with.

When engaging in conversations, be present. It's tempting to scan the room looking for the next person to talk to, but this can come off as dismissive. People are drawn to individuals who give them their full attention—it makes them feel valued and heard. Invest your attention fully in the interaction at hand, and the impression you'll leave will be one of genuine interest and respect.

It's also critical to be authentic. Authenticity resonates with people and builds trust. Tell stories about your experiences, share your passion for your work, and don't shy away from being vulnerable about the challenges you face. This not only humanizes you but also encourages others to open up and creates a deeper connection.

Additionally, positional authority isn't the only source of influence; relational influence is often cultivated in social settings. Pay attention to the dynamics of the room. Offering assistance or connecting two individuals who could benefit from knowing each other exemplifies leadership qualities and makes you a memorable presence.

Remember, networking is a two-way street. It's just as much about what you can offer as what you can gain. Approach every interaction with a mindset of service and think about how you can help others. This shift in perspective can alleviate some of the pressure to 'perform' and turns networking into a more natural and productive practice.

One of the many barriers women may face is the imposter syndrome, which can rear its head at social events. Combat these feelings by reflecting on your accomplishments and the unique perspective you bring to the table. You have earned your place in these spaces, and your contributions are valuable and necessary.

To keep the momentum going, follow up with the connections you've made. Send a personalized message referencing your conversation, propose a further meeting, or simply express your appreciation for the exchange. Timely follow-up demonstrates professionalism and solidifies the connection.

In walks resilience, a consistent theme in the pursuit of leadership. Not every event will go as planned, not every interaction will result in a valuable connection, and that's okay. Each social gathering is a learning experience, providing insights into what works and areas for improvement. Use these events as stepping stones, refining your approach as you progress.

And finally, reflect on each event and your performance. Celebrate your successes, no matter how small, and develop strategies for any areas where you feel you could improve. Continuous reflection and self-improvement are hallmarks of great leaders.

As you navigate social events with confidence, you not only expand your network but also reinforce your reputation as a leader. Each interaction is a brushstroke on the canvas of your career. With poise, authenticity, and the strategic tips discussed here, you're well on your way to painting a masterpiece of leadership success.

CHAPTER 8:
DECISION-MAKING WITH CONFIDENCE

As a leader, the power to make decisions is in your hands, and wielding that power with confidence sets the stage for success. Embracing the role of a decisive problem solver means understanding that hesitation can often be more detrimental than making an imperfect choice. This chapter serves as your guide to overcoming analysis paralysis, a common pitfall that hampers the decision-making process. You'll learn techniques for streamlining your problem-solving approach, ensuring that you're not only effective but also efficient in navigating the complex maze of leadership challenges. Acquiring the skill to make timely, informed decisions is pivotal; it instills trust in your team and asserts your leadership presence. As you immerse yourself in the strategies outlined, you'll find that your confidence as a decision-maker doesn't just grow—it thrives, empowering you to lead with both boldness and wisdom.

The Leader as Decisive Problem Solver

For those at the helm of organizations or teams, swift and effective decision-making is not just a skill; it's an essential part of the leadership fabric. As women aspiring to or occupying leadership positions, cultivating a decisiveness that's both respected and effective is paramount. Decisiveness in leadership is not merely about making quick decisions; it's about making the right decisions, at the right time, for the right reasons.

True leadership is tested in the face of problems. When challenges arise, teams look to their leaders for direction and assurance. As such, a leader's ability to solve problems decisively is a beacon of confidence and security for their team. In developing this skill, one first acknowledges that perfection isn't the goal. It's about informed action and unwavering commitment once a decision is made.

The journey to becoming a decisive problem solver begins with collating sufficient information. This involves researching, understanding the context, and gathering data before arriving at any conclusions. This process must be thorough but timely. There's a fine balance between making an uninformed decision and falling into the trap of over-analysis. Gathering diverse perspectives, especially from individuals with differing viewpoints, is invaluable in this phase.

After information gathering, it's vital to pivot to evaluation. Assess the potential outcomes of your decision—weigh the benefits and consider the risks. Employing tools like SWOT analysis (Strengths, Weaknesses, Opportunities, Threats) can streamline this process. Deciphering this landscape doesn't just bolster the leader's confidence in her decision; it reinforces the team's trust in her capability to lead.

Collaboration is another indispensable aspect of problem-solving. Engaging your team and stakeholders in the decision-making process not only fosters inclusion but also garners support and eases implementation. However, collaboration doesn't imply shying away from taking charge when necessary. As a leader, it's essential to elicit input while retaining the authority to make the final call.

Setting clear objectives provides a focus that aligns your team's efforts toward a common goal. With clear targets in mind, decisions can be more straightforward as they either move you towards or away from these objectives. This clarity allows for decisiveness as it filters out unrelated options and concentrates efforts where they matter most.

In problem-solving, creativity is a strength that cannot be undervalued. Out-of-the-box thinking can transform obstacles into opportunities. Encourage innovative solutions within your team and foster an environment where unconventional ideas are welcomed and explored. This may lead to novel approaches that traditional methods would have overlooked.

Risk-taking, within reasonable bounds, is inherent in leadership. Not every decision will have a guaranteed positive outcome. Sometimes, you'll need to make bold moves, knowing that there is no progress without some level of risk. As you navigate these waters, ensure that risks are calculated and that plans for mitigation are in place.

Flexibility in adjusting plans as new information arises is another hallmark of a decisive leader. Recognize that the landscape may change, and be prepared to adapt your strategy accordingly. This agility is not a sign of indecisiveness but a testament to a leader's responsiveness and resilience.

Once a decision is made, clear communication is pivotal. Articulate the rationale, the expected outcomes, and the steps that need to be taken to your team. Strong communication not only paves the way for seamless execution but also reinforces trust in your leadership.

Implementing your decisions with conviction is critical. Be proactive in leading the charge and set an example for your team. Show them that you stand firmly behind your decisions and are ready to navigate through their execution. This demonstration of commitment will often inspire the same level of dedication from your team members.

Reflection after the fact is as crucial as the decision-making process itself. Every decision, whether it results in success or requires further adjustment, is an opportunity for growth. Analyze the outcomes, learn from them, and use these insights to sharpen your decision-making skills for future challenges.

Developing a track record of solid decisions builds your reputation as a leader. It becomes part of your personal brand, fostering an image of reliability and intelligence. Your history of decisiveness will precede you, often making it easier to garner support and generate momentum for future initiatives.

Throughout this journey, remember that decisiveness is not just about making decisions for the sake of it. A decisive leader always aligns her actions with her values, the organization's mission, and the betterment of her team. The essence of your leadership is not defined by how often you decide, but by how well your decisions translate into positive outcomes and a path forward for everyone you lead.

In summary, becoming a decisive problem solver requires a mix of information mastery, clear communication, risk management, and adaptable execution. It's a dance between assertiveness and flexibility, logic and creativity, confidence and humility. As women leaders, embracing this role is instrumental in demonstrating that leadership is not just about occupying a position. It's about taking thoughtful, bold, and effective actions that cultivate progress and drive change.

Overcoming Analysis Paralysis

As women aspiring to leadership positions, you might have encountered the crippling grip of analysis paralysis—a state where the fear of making an incorrect decision leads to a cycle of overanalyzing, causing a breakdown in the decision-making process. But fear not; this section is dedicated to equipping you with strategies to break free from this cycle and step forward with confidence.

Firstly, it's important to acknowledge that analysis paralysis often stems from a desire for perfection and fear of failure. While striving for excellence is commendable, it's also vital to recognize that no leader is infallible. Embracing the possibility of imperfection is a stepping stone to decisive action.

Setting clear deadlines for decisions can create a sense of urgency that can cut through the fog of hesitation. Time constraints force us to prioritize the information we really need, rather than getting lost in endless possibilities. Allow yourself the space to think but also the discipline to act.

Another effective technique is to limit the influx of information. Too much data can be overwhelming, so focus on acquiring the critical details relevant to your decision. Learning to sift through vast quantities of information to find the jewels that will inform a wise choice is a skill that can be honed over time.

Embracing the concept of 'satisficing,' a term coined by economist Herbert Simon, is also key. This means seeking a decision that's good enough, rather than the elusive 'best' decision. Perfection doesn't exist in a dynamic business environment, and a satisfactory decision made in a timely manner often yields better results than a perfect decision made too late.

Don't underestimate the power of intuition. As a leader, you've honed your instincts through experiences and knowledge. Trusting your gut can provide a shortcut through the analytical maze to a clear course of action. Balance logic with intuition and you'll find a harmonious method for making decisions.

It's also helpful to remember that not every decision is set in stone. Some choices can be changed, tweaked, and improved upon with time. Viewing decisions as iterative can lessen the fear of making an irreversible mistake and encourage you to take the first step.

Another strategy is to delegate. As a leader, you're not alone in the decision-making process. Leverage the strength of your team by entrusting them with research and preliminary decisions. This collective approach can mitigate the pressure and bring diverse perspectives to the table, enriching the decision-making process.

Breaking the decision into smaller parts can also alleviate the weight of the process. Instead of approaching it as a monumental task, dissect it into manageable chunks. This will make the task less daunting and allow for progress in stages.

When you find yourself stuck, flip the scenario: consider the consequences of inaction. Sometimes, visualizing the cost of not deciding can be the catalyst you need to move forward. The reality is that stagnation can be more damaging than a less-than-perfect decision.

Practice makes permanent, so develop regular decision-making exercises. Start with low-stakes environments where the implications are minimal and build your way up. This kind of consistent practice will make decision-making a more natural part of your leadership style.

Seeking feedback can also provide reassurance and clarity. Engaging with mentors, colleagues, or even friends about your decision-making process can unveil alternative perspectives or confirm that you're on the right track. This inclusive approach stimulates growth and can bolster your confidence.

In times of uncertainty, develop scenarios to map out potential outcomes. This helps in visualizing the results of different choices and prepares you for various eventualities. By doing so, you condition your mind to handle the results of your decisions with poise, whatever they may be.

Remember, leadership is not just about making the right decisions; it's about making decisions right. It's about how you handle the outcomes, adjust strategies, and continue to move forward. By forging ahead with this belief, each choice becomes a learning opportunity that refines your leadership acumen.

In the face of analysis paralysis, reframe the narrative. It's not a sign of incompetence but a symbol of your dedication to excellence. With each step you take to overcome it, you show not just those around you, but yourself, that you are capable of confident, decisive action.

Through adopting these strategies to conquer analysis paralysis, you'll find that your leadership prowess will grow in tandem with your decision-making confidence. Each decision is a thread in the fabric of your legacy; make it strong, make it bold, and make it uniquely yours.

CHAPTER 9:
CONFLICT RESOLUTION AND INFLUENCE

Conflict in the workplace, if left unchecked, can unravel even the strongest of teams; however, friction also presents an opportunity for exceptional leadership to shine through. In "Conflict Resolution and Influence," we delve into the heart of navigating disputes with elegance and turning contention into a productive dialogue. You'll discover the gravity of maintaining composure when stakes are high and emotions run deep. Techniques for persuasive negotiation will be unveiled, empowering you to assert influence without coercion, fostering an atmosphere of mutual respect and understanding. The art of making peace with grace positions you not only as a leader but as an influential visionary equipped to build alliances from adversary moments. Providing strategies to defuse tensions and facilitate harmonious resolutions, this chapter is the blueprint for shaping outcomes that align with both your vision and values, setting a precedent for leadership that leaves a profound and positive impact.

Navigating Disputes with Finesse

In the nuanced world of leadership, conflicts aren't just obstacles to be resolved; they're opportunities to demonstrate finesse and to fortify relationships. As you navigate the tides of discord, remember that the heart of influence lies in understanding opposed perspectives and transforming contention into collaboration. Begin by actively listening, recognizing that the undercurrents of most disputes flow from unmet needs and expectations. Use questions to uncover these hidden drivers and to demonstrate genuine interest in finding a common ground. When articulating your own stance, be assertive yet empathetic, ensuring you're heard without diminishing the other party's viewpoint. A leader's mettle is tested not by her ability to levy fines or force compliance but through her skillful negotiation, fostering a culture of mutual respect. Crafting solutions that honor the interests of all parties doesn't merely solve the immediate conflict; it strengthens your reputation as an influential leader who guides with wisdom and integrity. Balance the scales with practicality and warmth, and you'll not only master the art of dispute resolution but will do so with a grace that inspires loyalty and fosters an environment where every team member can thrive.

Persuasion Techniques in Negotiation – As women poised for leadership, mastering the subtle art of persuasion in negotiation is a critical skill that will set you apart in any workplace. Understanding how to influence outcomes without coercion or manipulation can lead to successful and equitable agreements that bolster your leadership presence. In this chapter, we dive into the nuances of persuasion and how you can leverage certain techniques to tip the scales in your favor during negotiations.

Negotiation is not just about the give-and-take; it's about positioning yourself in a manner that the counterpart doesn't only hear but actively listens and engages with your proposals. The backbone of persuasive negotiating is built upon a deep understanding of one's own objectives, as well as those of the other party. Intertwining this knowledge seamlessly into the discourse can transform the nature of the negotiation.

One foundational persuasion technique is the principle of reciprocity. It's the idea that when someone does something for us, we naturally want to return the favor. In the context of negotiation, offering something of value--information, concessions, or understanding--can make the other side more inclined to reciprocate your gesture. It's not just about being fair; it's about creating a dynamic of mutual respect and exchange.

Then there's commitment and consistency — people want to act consistently with their commitments and values. Ensure that you're framing your side of the negotiation in a way that aligns with the other party's self-image or past decisions. If they've committed to quality and your solution is the highest quality, remind them. This congruency makes it psychologically easier for them to agree with you.

Social proof is another compelling tool. It involves using the power of the crowd to support your position. If others — especially those similar to your negotiating partner — are onboard with your idea, it's easier for your partner to agree.

They won't want to be left out of what is seen as the collective wisdom or trend.

Liking is perhaps one of the most underrated persuasion techniques. The simple truth is, we're more likely to agree with people we like. Building rapport and finding common interests will not only make the negotiation process more enjoyable but can also significantly impact the outcome. A friendly demeanor, a genuine smile, and active listening go a long way.

Authority is a powerful persuasive element. This doesn't mean you should tout your qualifications incessantly. However, demonstrating your expertise and competence can lead to your voice being taken more seriously. Cite data, share experiences, or introduce insights that showcase your authoritative knowledge on the subject at hand.

Scarcity can tilt the scales in your favor. The less there is of something, the more valuable it becomes. Skillfully communicate the unique benefits and the distinct scarcity of what you're offering, whether it's an opportunity, a partnership, or a product.

Anchoring is another negotiation tactic. Your initial proposal sets the stage for all subsequent negotiations. If you start strong—without being unreasonable—you give yourself more room to navigate and still achieve an outcome that you find satisfactory.

Framing is all about the lens through which a proposal is viewed. The same offer presented in different ways can lead to different reactions. It's important to frame your proposals in a positive light and to show how they align with the strategic objectives and personal aspirations of the other party.

The 'door-in-the-face' technique is a counterintuitive strategy where you begin with a large request, expecting a refusal, and then scale down to a smaller, more reasonable one. This smaller request now seems much more palatable in comparison and is more likely to be accepted.

Contrarily, the 'foot-in-the-door' technique starts with a small request—one that is almost impossible to refuse—and once it's granted, you follow with the larger request that you initially aimed to achieve. The agreement to the smaller request creates a bond that makes agreement to the larger one more likely.

Highly effective negotiators also use the 'yes, and...' approach. This is a technique borrowed from improv theater which promotes agreement and co-creation. When you're hit with an objection, acknowledge it with 'yes, and...' then pivot to add your viewpoint. This validates the other person's stance while also building on the conversation.

The power of silence shouldn't be underestimated. In a world where many are uncomfortable with silence, using it strategically can prompt the other party to fill the void, often with concessions or additional information that can be beneficial to you.

Lastly, don't forget the power of a well-placed question. Questions can guide your counterpart to think along the lines you want them to and can reveal their underlying interests and concerns, allowing you to tailor your approach for maximum persuasive impact. Open-ended questions can be especially powerful, as they encourage the other party to provide more information which you can use to your advantage.

Remember, the aim is to persuade, not to defeat. Successful negotiation is about finding a solution that is acceptable to all parties. It's about influence, not control. As you rise through the ranks of leadership, these techniques will be invaluable tools in your arsenal. They can help to ensure that your vision, and the needs of your team and organization, are represented and respected in every deal you're part of.

Maintaining Composure Under Pressure

When caught in the eye of a storm, the thriving leader stands unwavering, emulating a tranquility that quiets chaos itself. This is the essence of maintaining composure under pressure, an indispensable facet in the realm of conflict resolution and influence. The ability to remain serene and in control amid conflicts not only empowers you to navigate through disputes more effectively but also inspires confidence within your team.

Composure under pressure doesn't imply a lack of emotion or concern; on the contrary, it's about managing one's emotions constructively. It's common for leaders, especially women pursuing high-stakes roles, to face intense scrutiny and sometimes unfounded skepticism. Your response in such instances sets the tone for your leadership narrative.

To cultivate composure, start by acknowledging the physiological signs of stress. Your breath quickens, palms sweat, and heart races—all normal reactions. Recognize these signals and employ deep, mindful breathing to anchor your nervous system. With each breath, imagine drawing in calm and exhaling tension, much like a seasoned captain steadily guiding a ship through choppy waters.

Preparation is your ally. Familiarity with your environment, subject matter, and potential obstacles breeds confidence. When you've done the groundwork, pressure transforms from a foe to an acquaintance you know how to navigate. Developing a deep understanding of your business, your team, and the intricacies of the issues at hand instills an inner confidence that naturally deflates the pressure.

Visualization is a technique often used by successful leaders. Picture yourself handling a tense situation with poise and decisive action. What would you say? How would you stand? What solutions would you offer? These mental rehearsals prime you to perform under real-life pressure with the grace you've envisioned.

Effective communication is indispensable when the stakes are high. It's not just about what you say, but how you say it. Your voice should exude calm and authority, reassuring those around you. Practice speaking slowly and clearly, showing that you are not rushed by the pressure but are thoughtfully considering each step forward.

Don't underestimate the power of a pause. In high-pressure situations, a moment of silence can be profoundly strategic. It allows you to collect your thoughts, discourages panic, and conveys a sense of control. It signals to others that you're not flustered by the urgency of the moment but are contemplating a judicious response.

Another facet of maintaining composure is adaptability—the capacity to pivot when unforeseen challenges arise. A composed leader understands that no plan is infallible and being flexible in your approach is a strength, not a weakness. Being adaptable demonstrates that you can handle pressure without becoming rigid or overwhelmed.

Emotion regulation is crucial. Being aware of and managing your emotional responses ensures that they don't escalate and affect your decision-making process. This doesn't mean suppressing your emotions but rather understanding them. It's about recognizing the impact they have on you and maneuvering through them with intelligence and finesse.

In the midst of a conflict, remember to keep the bigger picture in focus. Fixating on minor details can increase anxiety and cloud judgment. By keeping your eyes on the overarching objectives and outcomes, you maintain the perspective necessary to stay composed and solutions-oriented.

Encounter every challenging situation as an opportunity for personal and professional growth. Remind yourself that pressure can actually enhance performance, forging you into a more resilient leader. It's in these very moments that you can demonstrate your capacity to rise above and inspire others to do the same.

Finally, surround yourself with a supportive network. Colleagues, peers, or mentors who can offer perspective during tough times are invaluable. They can provide a sounding board, share wisdom from their own experiences, and remind you of your capabilities when self-doubt seeks to creep in.

True composure is not about being unaffected by pressure—it's about how elegantly you dance with it. It's a blend of preparation, self-awareness, and confidence that tells the world, "I am capable." Remember, the most inspiring leaders are not those who never face adversity but those who handle it with an unshakable grace.

In the chapters that follow, we'll explore resilience, adaptive leadership, and the significance of fostering diverse teams. But for now, let this idea anchor you: composure is the silent symphony that orchestrates your influence during conflict—it's your hidden superpower, waiting to be mastered and unleashed. Step into your potential with the poise of a leader who knows that pressure isn't just a test, but a testament to her inner strength.

As you aspire to leadership greatness, reflect on the idea that maintaining composure under pressure isn't just a skill—it's a declaration of your leadership ethos. It's a testament to your preparedness to embrace challenges with elegance and to navigate the ever-changing tides of the workplace with an unshakeable calm. It's your moment to shine, to display the finesse of a leader who not only withstands the storm but also harnesses its energy to propel forward.

CHAPTER 10:
LEADING WITH RESILIENCE

Emerging from the thoughtful examination of conflict resolution in the previous chapter, we pivot to the heart of tenacity in leadership: resilience. In a world where setbacks are as certain as the sunrise, a leader's endurance isn't just about how she weathers storms but how she inspires her team to embrace the inevitability of change with courage. This chapter delves into the transformative power of resilience, exploring not only how to bounce back from personal and professional setbacks but also how to bolster a work culture that thrives on adaptability. We'll dissect the habits that resilient leaders practice daily and understand how they maintain their inner strength and keep their vision crystal clear, even when faced with the most challenging situations. By forging a path of resilience, you'll discover that the art of springing forward after a fall is more than recovery—it's a chance to emerge stronger, wiser, and with an infectious zeal that can galvanize your entire team.

Bouncing Back After Setbacks

Setbacks are an inevitable part of any leader's journey, yet how one responds to them can either fortify their resilience or undermine their effectiveness. Despite setbacks, a leader must demonstrate the powerful ability to rebound, turning obstacles into opportunities for growth. Within the domain of leadership, this chapter is devoted to exploring methods and strategies for bouncing back after facing adversities, challenges, or failures.

First and foremost, recognizing the setback openly is pivotal. As a woman vying for, or already in, a leadership position, you should not shy away from acknowledging the difficulties you face. Transparency about the challenges encountered not only humanizes your leadership but also invites your team to contribute to collective problem-solving efforts.

An integral aspect of bouncing back is the practice of self-reflection. Ask yourself critical questions. What can be learned from this experience? How has this challenge changed your perspective on leadership? Reflective thinking enables you to distill valuable lessons from setbacks that can enhance your leadership capability.

It's also crucial to maintain a positive but realistic mindset. Positivity alone isn't enough if it borders on denial. However, optimistic realism – a belief in eventual success tempered by an understanding of reality – fosters the resilience needed to overcome challenges.

After reflection, take decisive action. Develop a plan to address the setback directly. This might involve adjusting a project timeline, reevaluating objectives, or seeking additional support. Whatever the strategy, the point is to move forward with purpose and clarity.

Moreover, one shouldn't underestimate the power of a strong support network during tough times. Surround yourself with mentors, peers, and allies who can offer guidance, perspective, and encouragement. Fellow leaders, especially other women who have faced similar challenges, can offer invaluable support and advice.

Finding strength in vulnerability is also a key part of bouncing back. Sometimes, leaders feel they must conceal their struggles to maintain authority. However, showing vulnerability at the right time and in the right way can strengthen trust and loyalty in teams. It's a delicate balance to strike, but when done effectively, it can bolster your resilience and your team's.

Learning to prioritize and delegate are essential skills in the face of setbacks. Leaders must recognize their limits and share responsibilities to focus on recovery strategies. Delegation not only alleviates pressure but also empowers your team by entrusting them with important tasks.

Practicing self-care cannot be overstated. Leaders often sideline their well-being for the sake of the job, yet personal health is integral to professional performance. Whether it's physical exercise, meditation, or adequate rest, ensuring your well-being is a priority will better equip you to handle setbacks.

It's also valuable to study the setbacks of other leaders. History and biographies are replete with stories of women who faced and overcame significant obstacles. By learning how they navigated their difficulties, you can draw inspiration and adopt proven strategies in your own leadership journey.

Embrace adaptability as you work through setbacks. The world we lead in is dynamic and often unpredictable. The ability to pivot and adapt to changing circumstances is a hallmark of resilient leadership. Cultivating a mindset that is open to change can turn a setback into a stepping stone for innovation.

Finally, perseverance cannot be overlooked. Persistence in the face of adversity often defines the difference between a temporary failure and a permanent defeat. Leaders must cultivate the fortitude to continue pushing forward, even when progress seems slow or the outcome uncertain.

Celebrating small victories along the way is also vital. Acknowledging progress, no matter how incremental, can provide the motivation needed to overcome larger hurdles. Celebrate with your team and reinforce the message that every step forward is a success to be valued.

At times, however, it's possible that a setback might lead to recognizing when to let go of a failing strategy or initiative. This is not a sign of defeat, but rather an exercise in wisdom and strategic judgment. Knowing when to redirect efforts is a powerful aspect of resilient leadership.

Lastly, documenting your journey through setbacks not only serves as a personal reminder of your resilience but also can become a guide for others. Keeping a leadership journal where you note challenges, emotional responses, strategies employed, and lessons learned can be both therapeutic and instructive for future reference.

In the realm of leadership, resiliency isn't just about bouncing back; it's about bouncing forward, using setbacks as a catapult for growth and innovation. By integrating these strategies, you'll not only strengthen your ability to rebound from setbacks but also enhance your overall leadership presence and effectiveness.

Fostering a Culture of Adaptability

Leading with resilience isn't just a personal attribute; it's about cultivating an environment that supports and embodies flexibility and responsiveness, especially within the context of leadership. Adaptability is the cornerstone of a thriving workplace, particularly in our rapidly changing world. It is through this transformative lens that we will explore how to foster a culture that not only withstands change but thrives on it.

Adaptability in leadership means encouraging a growth mindset — a belief that skills and abilities can be developed through dedication and hard work. This approach nurtures potential and sees failure not as evidence of unintelligence but as a springboard for growth and for stretching our existing abilities. After all, when leaders display a growth mindset, their teams are more likely to embrace challenges and persist in the face of setbacks.

Embracing change is crucial in fostering adaptability. It means letting go of the 'we've always done it this way' mentality and instead, asking 'how can we improve?' Leaders must champion innovative thinking, which often means taking calculated risks and learning from the outcomes, regardless of whether they are successes or lessons.

Communication is vital in creating a culture of adaptability. As a leader, transparently sharing your vision for change, as well as the anticipated challenges and potential rewards, can galvanize your team. It's about creating an open dialogue where team members feel safe to voice their concerns, suggestions, and creative ideas.

Developing emotional intelligence goes hand in hand with adaptability. When you can understand and manage your emotions, as well as relate empathetically to others, you're more equipped to navigate the uncertain waters of change. This emotional agility allows leaders to provide the support their teams require during transitions.

Building a resilient team structure is also a part of fostering adaptability. This may include cross-training employees to perform multiple roles or encouraging a more project-based approach that allows for flexibility in team formations. When team members have a broader understanding of different parts of the business, they can more easily adapt to shifting needs.

Acknowledging and rewarding adaptable behavior is key. Recognize and celebrate when your team successfully navigates change or when an individual displays particularly flexible thinking or problem-solving. This not only boosts morale but reinforces the value placed on adaptability within the culture.

Curiosity and continuous learning are at the core of adaptive cultures. As a leader, you can model this by being an avid learner yourself and providing opportunities for your team's professional development. Encourage your team to explore new areas for learning and offer support for their educational endeavors.

Building trust is a fundamental element in adaptability. When team members trust the leadership and each other, they're more likely to buy into new ideas and methods. Creating a safe environment for experimentation allows your team to try new things without fear of repercussion if they don't yield the expected results.

Being proactive about change management is a responsibility of adaptable leaders. This involves anticipating potential scenarios and preparing your team for them. It's not just about reacting to changes as they come but being ahead of the curve where possible and having plans in place for different outcomes.

Leveraging technology can be an enabler of adaptability. Stay abreast of technological advancements that can improve efficiency, open up new channels of communication, or create novel ways to solve problems. Empower your team with the right tools to adapt to and embrace new solutions.

Empowerment is a powerful tool in fostering an adaptable culture. When team members feel empowered to make decisions and take action, they become more engaged and invested in the outcomes. As a leader, delegate authority and trust your team to make decisions aligned with the organization's goals.

Encouraging diversity of thought is critical to adaptability. When you bring together people with varying perspectives, it enriches the pool of ideas and fosters innovation. It requires an openness to challenge your own perspectives and to consider new and sometimes unconventional ideas.

Lastly, to foster a culture of adaptability, you must practice what you preach. Your behavior sets the tone for the rest of the team. Display adaptability in your actions, and your team is likely to follow suit. Show that you're committed to adapting to new challenges, and your team will imbibe that commitment into their work ethos.

In conclusion, fostering a culture of adaptability in the workplace is an ongoing process that requires commitment, communication, and a willingness to evolve. By embodying these principles and practices, you can lead your team with resilience and agility, paving the way for a dynamic, robust, and future-ready organization. Remember, as a leader, your actions and attitudes are the catalyst for change—embrace adaptability, and you'll inspire others to do the same.

CHAPTER 11:
BUILDING AND LEADING DIVERSE TEAMS

Transitioning from the individual resilience highlighted in the previous chapter, we now delve into the richness of diversity that defines the contemporary workplace. In this chapter, building and leading diverse teams becomes your platform for innovation, creativity, and organizational excellence. Imagine a tapestry, vibrant with varied threads, each contributing a unique strength; this is what you're weaving within your team. As a leader, your task is twofold: to identify and appreciate the individual differences that each member brings to the ensemble and to mold these distinct personalities, cultural backgrounds, and talents into a cohesive unit that outperforms the sum of its parts. You'll learn to bridge gaps not with mere tolerance, but with a genuine understanding and celebration of diversity, creating an environment where everyone feels valued and driven to contribute. The symphony of voices, when conducted with finesse, can harmonize into a narrative of success, becoming your team's most formidable asset. So, let's embark on this journey—embrace the complexities, champion inclusion, and let the diversity of your team be your guiding star to leadership excellence.

Valuing and Leveraging Differences

Understanding the rich tapestry of human experience is essential as you embark on building and leading diverse teams. The different perspectives, backgrounds, and abilities each member brings to the table are not merely factors to acknowledge; they are assets to value deeply and leverage strategically.

Diversity goes beyond the visible differences of race, gender, and age — it extends to the varied experiences, skills, thought processes, and cultural insights that each team member holds. When you as a leader value these differences, you set the stage for a vibrant, innovative, and competitive team environment.

Leveraging differences isn't just about creating a feel-good atmosphere. It's about capitalizing on the diverse set of ideas to push creativity, find unique solutions to challenges, and ultimately drive better business outcomes. By acknowledging each member's unique contributions, you foster an environment where individuals feel heard, respected, and motivated.

Begin by actively seeking out and recognizing varied viewpoints. Encourage participation and showcase different perspectives during team meetings. This not only enriches the decision-making process but also signals to the team that you place high value on diverse input.

Consider adapting your leadership style to various team members by understanding their personal work preferences and motivations. A one-size-fits-all approach can overlook the individual strengths that come with diversity. Tailoring your leadership to individuals' needs demonstrates that you value their uniqueness, which can lead to increased team loyalty and productivity.

Create opportunities for collaboration that purposefully mix different skill sets and backgrounds. Often, the most innovative solutions arise when people with different ways of thinking come together to address a common issue.

Be aware of unconscious biases that can sneak into the workplace. These deeply ingrained assumptions can undermine the value of diversity. Challenge your own preconceptions and work actively to mitigate biases in your team. Provide training and resources to help everyone understand and overcome these obstacles.

When conflicts arise from differences, view them as growth opportunities rather than setbacks. Facilitate open, respectful dialogue where all parties can express their views and work towards mutual understanding. Remember that constructive conflict, handled correctly, can lead to breakthrough ideas and strengthen team cohesion.

Set the example by being inclusive in language and actions. Ensure that your communication is clear, transparent, and culturally sensitive, creating an inclusive atmosphere where everyone feels they belong.

Recognize and celebrate cultural events and milestones that may be significant to various team members. This not only shows respect for individual backgrounds but also enriches the cultural fabric of the team.

Invest in ongoing diversity and inclusion training for yourself and your team members. This journey doesn't end with hiring practices; it's an ongoing process of learning and growth that requires commitment and intentional action.

Foster mentorship programs that connect employees from different backgrounds. This can enhance understanding and respect across the team while providing individual career development and networking opportunities.

Evaluate team performance with a focus on diversity outcomes. Track how effectively you are leveraging differences to meet your objectives, and adjust strategies as necessary to harness the full potential of your team's diversity.

Finally, remember that the practice of valuing and leveraging differences is a transformational journey. It's a continuous process of self-improvement and cultural evolution both for you as a leader and for your team. Stay steadfast in your commitment, and you will cultivate a team that not only achieves greatness but also embodies the principles of diversity and inclusion you champion.

By building upon the diverse experiences and ideas of each individual, you're not only leading a team – you're orchestrating a symphony of collective intelligence that can propel your organization to new heights. So value every note, capitalize on every rhythm, and create a masterpiece of leadership that resonates with the sound of true diversity and inclusion.

Inclusive Leadership Practices

Leading diverse teams is not simply about bringing together people from various backgrounds and hoping for the best; it involves an active commitment to creating an inclusive environment where every member can thrive. As women aspiring to leadership positions, you must constantly refine your skills to foster inclusivity. This chapter draws upon the importance and practices of inclusive leadership within diverse teams.

Inclusive leadership begins with self-awareness. Understanding your own biases, strengths, and weaknesses is paramount. Reflect on your interactions: Are you truly listening to different perspectives? Do you challenge your preconceptions? Self-awareness is the first step toward building a foundation of trust and respect in your team.

Communication is the bridge that connects varied experiences within a diverse team. Inclusive leaders are skilled at adapting their communication style to ensure that every team member feels heard and understood. This might mean taking the time to learn about cultural norms or being mindful of the language you use. Remember, it's not just what you say; it's how you say it— your tone, your body language, and your willingness to engage in difficult conversations with empathy and openness.

Inclusivity also means embracing and encouraging different ways of thinking within your team. When brainstorming or problem-solving, actively seek out and celebrate unique perspectives. This not only leads to better ideas but also strengthens team members' sense of belonging and value.

Decision-making processes must be transparent and equitable. Involve your team in the decisions that affect their work and their professional growth. When members see that their input has a real impact, they'll feel a greater sense of ownership and commitment to the team's objectives.

One of the most profound ways to demonstrate inclusivity is through mentorship. As a leader, be proactive in identifying and nurturing talent from within your team—especially those who may be underrepresented or marginalized. Your guidance can make a significant difference in someone's career and life.

Accountability goes hand in hand with leadership. Set clear expectations for respectful interactions within your team, and do not shy away from addressing issues of exclusion or discrimination swiftly and seriously. A strong leader does not tolerate behaviors that undermine the team's integrity.

Recognition is a powerful tool to promote inclusivity. Acknowledge the achievements and efforts of all team members. Public recognition not only boosts morale but also shows that you value diverse contributions. Ensure that rewards and promotions are based on merit and that there's a fair process in place for determining these.

Creating inclusive policies and practices isn't a one-time effort—it's an ongoing process that requires dedication and adaptability. Stay current with best practices in diversity and inclusion, and be willing to revise your approach in response to new insights or changing team dynamics.

An inclusive culture is very much about creating a space where different life experiences and worldviews are not just accepted but seen as a strength. Celebrate cultural events, acknowledge different holidays, and create opportunities for team members to share their traditions and stories. When people feel that their whole selves are welcome, they will invest more wholeheartedly in their work and the team.

Feedback is critical on your journey as an inclusive leader. Encourage and genuinely consider feedback from team members on how you can improve the inclusivity of your team. This might involve anonymous surveys, one-on-one meetings, or regular check-ins to ensure everyone's voice is heard and valued.

Leadership is not about having all the answers—it's about being open to learning. Inclusivity is a complex subject, and even the most well-intentioned leaders can make mistakes. When you do, own up to them, learn from them, and move forward with deeper understanding and compassion.

Inclusive leadership is not a passive stance; it is a dynamic, positive force for change. By cultivating a team that feels appreciated for their diversity, you create a vibrant, innovative, and resilient work environment that stands as a testament to the power of inclusivity in driving success.

As you build and lead diverse teams, remember that your role as a leader goes beyond managing tasks and meeting targets—it's about nurturing a community of professionals who feel supported and inspired to reach their full potential. Your efforts in practicing inclusive leadership will pave the way for a more equitable and effective workplace, creating a ripple effect that extends far beyond your team.

Thus, embracing and executing inclusive leadership practices is more than a strategic advantage—it is a commitment to excellence and integrity in leadership that acknowledges the dignity, value, and potential of every team member. As you continue on your leadership path, let inclusivity be the guiding principle that shapes your actions, strengthens your team, and defines your legacy.

CHAPTER 12:

PLANNING FOR PROGRESSION

As we forge ahead, it's crucial to understand that your leadership journey is an evolving process, one where strategic planning lights the path to success. In "Planning for Progression," we align the aspirational with the actionable, carving a clear trajectory for your career advancement. Imagine setting goals that not only challenge but excite you—objectives that nurture your growth and enable you to scale new heights. This chapter is a blueprint for mapping out your staircase to the stars. We'll delve into how you can define objectives that resonate with who you are and who you aim to become as a leader. It's about the commitment to continuous improvement and being proactive in seeking opportunities that expand your horizons. By the end of this chapter, you won't just be reaching for your next milestone; you'll be strategically equipping yourself for a career journey that blossoms with your evolving definition of leadership excellence. Brace yourself to craft a long-term vision with flexibility at its core, predicated on the tenet that progression is not just about climbing the ladder; it's about building a ladder that's uniquely yours.

Setting Achievable Leadership Goals

As you step into the realm of potential and progress, setting achievable leadership goals becomes the cornerstone of your professional trajectory. It's about striking that sweet balance between ambition and realism, where goals serve as stepping stones rather than hurdles. Start small; pinpoint the skills you're eager to refine or the knowledge you're looking to acquire, and give these aspirations timelines that challenge yet respect your current commitments. Remember, leadership isn't simply a title; it's an ongoing journey of growth. So, tailor your objectives to cultivate the kind of influence that not only shines today but also shapes a legacy. This could be enhancing your public speaking prowess, mastering conflict resolution, or driving innovative projects. Whatever your aims, ensure they are SMART: Specific, Measurable, Achievable, Relevant, and Time-bound. This approach will keep your progress palpable and your victories in clear sight, propelling you forward with conviction and a blueprint for success that matches the leader you're becoming.

Crafting a Long-Term Career Vision forms the backbone of any ambitious journey toward leadership. A career vision is like a compass that guides you through the unpredictable terrain of professional development, helping you to stay focused on your end goals and make strategic decisions along the way. For women aspiring to climb the leadership ladder, envisioning where you want to be in the long-term is not only motivational but essential.

A clear and compelling career vision empowers you to steer your growth in the right direction. It's about knowing what you're working toward and why it's important to you. Start by asking yourself what leadership looks like in your context. Is it about achieving a certain title, impacting a specific industry, or creating a legacy? Reflect deeply on what leadership and success mean to you personally, outside of societal norms and expectations.

After defining what leadership means to you, identify the values that are non-negotiable on your path. Integrity, innovation, and inclusivity may be among the core values you wish to embody. Remember, your career vision should align with your personal values, as authenticity in leadership is magnetic and fosters trust and respect from your peers and subordinates.

Consider the legacies of great women leaders you admire. What can you learn from their paths, and how can their journeys inform your own vision? Crafting your vision isn't about imitating others, but rather drawing inspiration and understanding how resilience, determination, and strategic planning can influence your own trajectory.

Set long-term goals that excite and challenge you. These should push you out of your comfort zone while still being attainable. For example, aim to lead a particular project, to be recognized with an industry award, or to reach a significant milestone in terms of your team's growth and performance.

It's vital to visualize your goals. Imagine stepping into the role you aspire to — what does it look and feel like? Visualization is a powerful tool that can boost your motivation and commitment to reaching your goals. It creates a mental picture that's hard to shake and something to strive for every day. Can you see yourself leading meetings, giving keynote speeches, or mentoring the next generation of leaders?

Break your long-term vision down into medium and short-term goals. This makes your vision more tangible and actionable. For instance, if your vision is to become a CEO, medium-term goals might include obtaining an MBA or mastering the financial aspects of your business. Short-term goals might then focus on taking on projects that increase your visibility and understanding of different parts of your current organization.

Write your vision down. Documenting your vision adds a level of commitment and clarity. It becomes a tangible reference you can come back to, refine, and evaluate over time. Keep it somewhere you can see it regularly, so it stays at the forefront of your mind and influences your daily actions and decisions.

Seek feedback on your vision. Discussing your career vision with trusted mentors or peers can provide new insights and help you refine your goals. Feedback can also lead to uncovering opportunities that align with your vision, which you might not have discovered on your own.

Be prepared to adapt your vision over time. As industries evolve and personal growth occurs, what you want in the long-term may change. Flexibility is a leadership trait that demonstrates your ability to adjust while keeping your eyes on the big picture. Your career is a living, dynamic journey, not set in stone.

Remember, crafting a long-term career vision is just one component of your professional growth. Setting the vision lays the groundwork for further development, networking, decision-making capabilities, and conflict resolution skills—all necessary for an illustrious leadership career. These components are interwoven and each will be explored in depth throughout other sections of this book.

Don't underestimate the importance of continuous learning and development in service of your vision. Gaining new skills and knowledge not only makes you more qualified for future roles but also shows a commitment to your career that can set you apart from others. It's a clear sign that you're invested in your path and proactive about your growth.

Above all, your career vision should inspire you. It should resonate with your deepest ambitions and push you to bring your best self to your professional life. Having a vision isn't about plotting out every step with certainty; it's about establishing a direction that guides the choices you make and the opportunities you pursue.

Fueling your journey with passion, cultivating resilience, and embracing the twists and turns along the way will pave the path to fulfilling your vision. The climb to leadership can be steep at times, but with a clear vision, relentless determination, and a commitment to learning and adapting, you'll reach heights that perhaps once felt impossible. This vision is your narrative of potential—the story of the leader you're destined to become.

So, as you contemplate your long-term career vision, approach it not just as a checklist of achievements, but as a living statement of your leadership aspirations. Let it grow with you, guide you through challenges, and celebrate your wins. Your career vision is the extraordinary possibility of what you can accomplish—it's the blueprint for the leader you will be.

Continuous Learning and Development

As you navigate the path of professional development, it is essential to realize that the pinnacle of leadership isn't a final destination. It's the steadfast commitment to continuous learning and development that distinguishes truly remarkable leaders from the rest. As you chart your journey forward, remember that the landscape of leadership is constantly evolving, and to remain relevant and effective, so too must you.

Commitment to life-long education is a hallmark of success, and it is particularly pressing in the fluid world of leadership. You must strive to stay ahead of the curve, not only in your specific field but also in the areas that contribute to broad-based leadership skills, such as emotional intelligence, strategic thinking, and negotiation.

Foster a mindset of growth that seeks out knowledge and challenges preconceptions. Cultivating this mindset means more than attending seminars or earning certificates; it's about opening yourself up to new experiences and insights on a daily basis. Explore books, podcasts, and thoughtful discussion that expand your understanding of not just what it is to be a leader, but also what it means to be a leader in your particular sphere and beyond.

The pursuit of continuous learning is not a solo endeavor. To excel, you must seek out mentors and coaches who can provide guidance and feedback tailored to your unique circumstances. Engaging in respectful and meaningful dialogue with these individuals can help you fine-tune your skills and make significant strides in your leadership capabilities.

Engage actively with professional groups and networks that can offer support, advice, and camaraderie. Through these connections, you open yourself to the collective wisdom of peers who can challenge you, encourage you, and often help you see solutions and opportunities you might otherwise miss.

Set aside time for reflection to truly internalize and apply what you learn. Reflective practice is vital in transforming new knowledge into practical wisdom. Ask yourself critical questions about your experiences and find ways to incorporate the insights gained into your leadership style and decision-making processes.

Be fearless in the pursuit of knowledge. It can sometimes feel uncomfortable to delve into areas where your expertise is less secure, but that discomfort is a sign of growth. The best leaders are those who aren't afraid to step outside their comfort zones to enhance their understanding and skills.

Embrace technology and digital platforms that facilitate learning. In today's digital age, access to knowledge is at your fingertips. Utilize online courses, webinars, and interactive platforms to dive deeper into subjects that interest you and those that will boost your competencies as a leader.

Continuing education and professional development courses should also be a part of your regular routine. These structured learning opportunities can not only add to your repertoire of skills but also provide a framework for tackling new challenges that you might encounter in your career.

Be an advocate for the development of others. The process of teaching and mentoring can itself be an enriching experience that reinforces your own understanding and beliefs about leadership. The act of helping others progress in their careers will also help you to gain perspective and learn from their journeys.

Encourage a culture of development and learning within your team and organization. As a leader, your attitude towards learning can have a significant impact on those around you. By modeling a commitment to personal growth, you inspire your team members to emulate the same behaviors, which in turn, can elevate the entire organization.

Utilize self-assessment tools and solicit feedback regularly to gauge your development. Understanding where you currently stand can help you set more targeted learning goals and strategies, enhancing your chances of achieving them.

Nurture a variety of interests outside your professional sphere. Diverse experiences can contribute to a more well-rounded perspective on leadership, benefiting your approaches to management, innovation, and problem-solving in unexpected ways.

Finally, remember that your learning and development journey is uniquely yours. What works for one person may not work for another, and it is important to find the approaches—that blend of reading, dialogue, practice, and reflection—that suit you best. Be patient with yourself through the process, knowing that personal development is an ongoing cycle of achieving mastery, reassessing goals, and pushing beyond current limits.

Prepare to enrich your career and elevate your leadership potential through a lifelong dedication to learning and growth. With the strategies and mindsets outlined, your journey of continuous development will not only lead to greater personal success but will also empower you to uplift others, fostering progress throughout your sphere of influence and beyond.

YOUR LEADERSHIP LEGACY

As we draw close to the end of this transformative journey, the focus shifts to a horizon that's yours and yours alone—your leadership legacy. Unlike the chapters that paved the way, filled with strategies and practices for enhancing your presence, mastering communication, building resilience, and fostering inclusivity, this final chapter isn't about the tools for the job. Instead, it's about the mark you make with them.

What do you want to be remembered for? This question isn't just rhetorical. It's the driving force behind every decision and every relationship you cultivate as a leader. Your legacy is more than just a byproduct of your leadership; it's the culmination of your purpose, your values, and the impact you make. It echoes in the corridors of your organization long after you've moved on, residing in the success of the teams you've empowered and the changes you've enacted.

A leader's legacy is not crafted from titles or the accolades that gather dust on a shelf. Rather, it's woven into the fabric of your organization's culture. It's reflected in the ways your colleagues speak about you, the policies you put in place, and the collective grit and grace with which your team confronts challenges. The real metric of your influence is how well the garden grows when you're not there to tend it.

Building your legacy requires you to be intentional—every word you utter, every barrier you dismantle, every hand you extend in support adds a strand to the tapestry of your ultimate remembrance. Make use of the strategies outlined earlier in this text, but infuse them with the authenticity that can come only from you. The passion and conviction you hold for your vision are contagious; infect others with the drive to achieve collective excellence.

Take heart in knowing that leadership is as much about serving as it is about directing. Your legacy will be the stories of those you elevated, the voices you amplified—those who stood tall because you provided the pedestal of support and empowerment. In the end, your legacy will be defined by the growth and achievements of others just as much as your own.

Remember that the journey of leadership is one of continual evolution. The close of this book is not the end—it's simply a checkpoint on your pathway to greatness. Gaze confidently into the future with the assurance that the skills, insights, and experiences you've gained are the foundation of the great legacy you're destined to leave.

As the final page turns, pause to envision the leader you have become through diligence and determination. Cast your gaze forward and imagine the leader you are still yet to be. Stand tall, take a deep breath, and step forward with a clear vision. Your leadership legacy isn't a static monument but an ongoing narrative of empowerment and excellence that will inspire the next generation of women leaders who follow in your footsteps. Go forth and craft a legacy that is not only lasting but luminous.

APPENDIX A:
POWER POSE
PRACTICE EXERCISES

Having journeyed through the nuances of cultivating a compelling leadership presence, it's time to put theory into action. These practice exercises will help you embody the confidence and assertiveness needed to make your mark as a leader. Let's dive in to some power pose practice to manifest your leadership skills from the outside in.

Exercise One: The Superwoman Stance

Start by standing tall, feet shoulder-width apart. Plant your feet firmly on the ground, feel a rooted connection to the earth. As you draw your shoulders back, open up your chest proudly. Place your hands on your hips, take a deep breath in, and hold this pose for two minutes. Envision yourself ready to face any challenge, exuding unwavering strength and resolve. Let this pose remind you of your inner power.

Exercise Two: The Victory V

Inspired by the universal gesture for triumph, this pose is all about celebrating your wins, no matter how small. Sit or stand with your back straight, and reach your arms overhead into a V shape. As you breathe deeply, savor the feeling of accomplishment and allow it to bolster your confidence. Hold this position for one to two minutes, and let the sensation of success permeate your being.

Exercise Three: The Tabletopper

This pose can be done seated or standing and is perfect for assertively marking your territory in a meeting. Place your hands on the table, fingers spread wide, and lean slightly forward. This expansive gesture exudes control and dominion over the space and conversation. Maintain this assertive posture while you articulate your ideas with clarity and conviction.

Exercise Four: The Listener's Lean

Power isn't just about speaking; it's also about being an engaged and attentive listener. Sit at the edge of your chair with your feet flat on the floor and lean slightly forward, directed towards the speaker. Maintain eye contact and nod subtly to show understanding. This poised engagement not only conveys your interest but also establishes your presence in the dialogue.

Exercise Five: The Grounded Leader

To find balance and composure in moments of stress, plant your feet firmly on the ground, whether you're sitting or standing. Take a moment to feel the floor beneath you, draw up strength from it, and take slow, purposeful breaths. Enclose your fingers lightly in front of you or rest them on your thighs. Use this centered stance to reground yourself whenever you need to tap back into your leadership energy.

Integrating these power poses into your daily routine will gradually shift the way you carry yourself and how others perceive you. Remember that your body language speaks volumes before you even utter a word. Through these exercises, you'll start embracing a physicality that broadcasts your competence and readiness to lead. May your posture always reflect your emerging legacy of powerful, transformative leadership.

APPENDIX B:
RESOURCES FOR FURTHER LEARNING

As you've journeyed through this book, you've uncovered the nuances of leadership presence and began to harness the power within you to become a transformative leader. Continuing on your path to growth and excellence, it's vital to seek out further learning opportunities. Below is a curated selection of resources fundamental to broadening your horizon as a leader. These tools are chosen to inspire you, challenge you, and support your commitment to becoming an outstanding leader in the workplace.

Books

Books are a gateway to the minds of great leaders and thinkers. Explore works that delve deeper into leadership strategies, emotional intelligence, and much more:

- *Lean In: Women, Work, and the Will to Lead* by Sheryl Sandberg – This book offers insight into the challenges women face on the path to leadership and provides practical advice on how to overcome them.

- *Dare to Lead: Brave Work. Tough Conversations. Whole Hearts.* by Brené Brown – Brown shares her research into leadership and what it means to lead with vulnerability and courage.

- *The Confidence Code: The Science and Art of Self-Assurance – What Women Should Know* by Katty Kay and Claire Shipman – Learn about the importance of confidence and how it intersects with leadership for women.

Online Courses

Expand your knowledge and skills with online courses that can be conveniently accessed to fit your busy schedule:

1. Harvard's **Exercising Leadership: Foundational Principles** – A course that helps you understand the complexities of leadership and how to mobilize others.
2. Udemy's **Women in Leadership: Inspiring Positive Change** – Offers tools and strategies specifically for women looking to lead effectively in the workplace.
3. Coursera's **Inspirational Leadership: Leading with Sense** – Focuses on becoming a leader who inspires and empowers others to achieve their best.

Podcasts

Podcasts can be a great way to learn while on the move. Listen to the experiences of successful leaders from various fields:

- *HBR's Women at Work* – Conversations about the workplace, and women's place in it.
- *Leading with Purpose* – Stories and practical advice from leaders making a difference.

- *The Leadership Pod* – Interviews and discussions on leadership challenges and triumphs.

Networking Groups and Forums

Engaging with a community of like-minded individuals can provide support, mentorship, and new opportunities:

1. Lean In Network – Connect with a global community of women in leadership, offering circles for regular meetups and exchange of ideas.
2. Ellevate Network – A community of professional women committed to helping each other succeed.
3. Women in Leadership Forum – Engage in discussions about leadership issues through webinars and events.

Remember, the pursuit of leadership excellence is an ongoing process that benefits from a commitment to continuous learning. The resources listed above are starting points; let them fuel your curiosity and lead you to discover additional materials that resonate with your leadership journey.

Take pride in each step you take. Remember that every leader's path is distinct. Embrace the unique insights and perspectives you bring to the table, and let them guide you as you carve out your own leadership legacy. With these resources at your side, you're well-equipped to lead with confidence, passion, and purpose.

www.ingramcontent.com/pod-product-compliance
Lightning Source LLC
Chambersburg PA
CBHW060110260726
48658CB00004B/1493